THE OIL RUSH

TEXT BY MERVYN JONES
PHOTOGRAPHY BY FAY GODWIN

QUARTET BOOKS LONDON

ALSO BY MERVYN JONES

Fiction
No Time to be Young
The New Town
The Last Barricade
Helen Blake
On the Last Day
A Set of Wives
John and Mary
A Survivor
Joseph
Mr Armitage Isn't Back Yet*
The Revolving Door*

Holding On*
Strangers*
Lord Richard's Passion*
The Pursuit of Happiness*
Scenes from Bourgeois Life*

Non-fiction
Potbank: A Study of the Potteries
Big Two: Aspects of America and Russia
Two Ears of Corn: Oxfam in Action
Life on the Dole

ALSO BY FAY GODWIN
The Oldest Road:
an exploration of the Ridgeway
(with J. R. L. Anderson)

* Available in Quartet editions

First published by Quartet Books Limited 1976
27 Goodge Street, London W1P 1FD

Text copyright © 1976 by Mervyn Jones

Photographs copyright © 1976 by Fay Godwin

designed by Mike Jarvis

Photographs printed by Adrian Holmes

ISBN 0 704 33095 4

Printed in Great Britain by litho by The Anchor Press Ltd
and bound by Wm Brendon & Son Ltd
both of Tiptree, Essex

PHOTOGRAPHER'S NOTE

The words and the images in this book are
different comments, each reinforcing and
adding to the other. Together, I hope that they
illustrate more than each could on its own.

Several times I was refused permission to make
trips to rigs, platforms, pipelaying barges and
other facilities, because I am a woman. All the
more thanks, therefore, to the firms which did not
refuse permission despite that fact.

The photographs were taken during the heatwave
in August 1975.

I would like to acknowledge the assistance and
co-operation of BP Ltd, Brown & Root (UK) Ltd,
Conoco (UK) Ltd, Hamilton Bros. Oil Company
(GB) Ltd, Shell (UK) Ltd and Wilhelm
Wilhelmsen, and I would especially like to thank
Beverly Sissons for all her help and hospitality.

BLACK GOLD

There was once – in an America that was still mainly rural, in the days before the Civil War – a dealer in quack medicines. He had two sons, and whilst they were still boys they showed their eagerness to learn the skills of business. In his own fashion, he trained them. He is recorded to have said:

'I cheat my boys every chance I get. I want to make 'em sharp. I trade with the boys and skin 'em and I just beat 'em every time I can.'

The name of this loving parent was Rockefeller. In 1860 his elder son, John D., made his way to western Pennsylvania. Here a sticky black liquid seeped out of the ground whenever a farmer dug a hole – oil. For some years it had been bottled and

Loch Kishorn
construction site

sold under the name of Keir's Medicine, but word was spreading that it was more valuable as a lubricant for railway engines and other new machines, or when made into paraffin and kerosene. Indeed, as the United States began to change from an agrarian into an industrial economy, oil was urgently needed. Derricks were springing up all over Pennsylvania's hills and valleys. The world's first oil rush had begun.

John D. Rockefeller became the monarch of the oilfields. He traded with the hundreds of small producers and skinned them and just beat them. Within a decade his company, Standard Oil, controlled every aspect of the oil business: extraction, refining and, by collusion with the railways, transport to the urban markets. When he officially retired from business in 1893, he had a personal fortune of $200 million; but he had divided his wealth with his brother and a variety of associates and nominees, and a well-informed broker said: 'John D. Rockefeller is worth a billion.' Already, oil had earned its name of 'black gold'.

In little more than a century, the demand for oil has increased to an extent that even the calculating Rockefeller could never have foreseen. It was thought to be tremendous by the 1920s, when the oil-driven ship, the car and the aeroplane had arrived; but since that time it has been multiplied forty times. The world now consumes 2,800 million tons of oil a year. Since it isn't easy for most of us to visualize a ton of oil, let me add that this is 686,000 million gallons. People generally think of oil in connection with their cars, but only a fifth of the oil used by an industrial country takes the form of petrol. Primarily, oil is the machine-driving fuel in countless factories; oil-fuelled power stations and domestic heating also make a significant contribution. As well as this, oil is the raw material for all kinds of substances, notably plastics, so that the petrochemical industry has become a thriving child of its gargantuan parent.

With America in the van, and European nations following in recent decades, oil has been sweeping aside its competitors. In 1950 it supplied only 10% of Britain's energy. By 1970 its share had risen to 44%, with coal at 47% and the balance going to natural gas, hydro-electric power and nuclear energy. Very soon after this book is published, we shall be dependent on oil for more than half of our fuel needs.

If oil were produced by the same countries that consume it, it would be a factor in national but not in international politics. However, the reality is very different – except in the Communist world, where the Soviet Union balances production and consumption at a figure of rather more than 400 million tons, and China also seems to have enough for her needs. The United States, with rich oilfields in Texas and California, was self-sufficient well into the twentieth century; but by 1973, though still the world's leading producer with 456 million tons, it was consuming 814 million. Western Europe, consuming 747 million, produces a mere 22 million from small oilfields in France, Germany and Austria. Japan needs 267 million tons and produces none at all.

Nations such as Britain began to need (or want) oil in significant quantities at a time when they were accustomed to taking what they sought. They found it in countries that were either imperial possessions or, if legally independent, too weak to resist the unrewarded exploitation of their resources. First to yield the 'black gold' were Persia and Mesopotamia – as Iran and Iraq were then called – and Burma. The Anglo-Persian Oil Company, which has become British Petroleum, was the main entrepreneur. Royal Dutch Shell, with capital and directors drawn from both Britain and the Netherlands, opened up Indonesia (part of the Dutch Empire) and then found a bonanza in Venezuela. Except for Burma, which has disappeared from the oil map, these are still big producers. Iran had an output in 1973 of 293 million tons, Venezuela 179 million, Indonesia 64 million.

Since the last war, United States dependence on imported oil has spurred American companies – such as Exxon, the modern name for Standard Oil – to open up new fields in the Middle East. Indeed, it seemed that fresh oil-bearing regions could be discovered and tapped as fast as they were needed. Saudi Arabia by 1973 was producing 364 million tons, Kuwait 138 million, Libya 105 million, Nigeria 100 million. In one country after another, just as long ago in rural Pennsylvania, the oil rush changed the visible landscape and the economic scene out of recognition within a few years. Strangers built self-contained cities, little fishing harbours became flourishing ports, huge profits were banked far away.

But will there always be more oil awaiting the exploration teams? There has been, so far; in 1919 the United States was warned by its Government that it would use up all its oil within thirty years, at a rate of consumption tiny by later standards, and the oil is still flowing. It is true that oilfields are usually bigger – both richer and more extensive – than could be assumed from the first surveys. Estimates of Middle East reserves, both known and probable, are constantly on the increase. It is also true that oil is being pumped from the depths and literally burned at a phenomenal and one must surely say a reckless rate; appeals for conservation have about as much effect as appeals to give up smoking. The ecologists may not be right in saying that the world will run out of oil within the next hundred years, but they must be right sooner or later.

Here a new thought occurs to the optimists. Oil is a hydrocarbon secreted in very ancient rocks, formed anything up to 300 million years ago; it is found at much greater depths than coal or copper or gold. It was there, in fact, before the geography of the continents took its present shape. Therefore, most of the oil must be under the sea, since most of the earth's surface is covered by water. It could be anywhere. Geologists can make intelligent guesses by studying coastal rock formations. Very probably, there is oil off northern Canada and Alaska, oil off Australia, oil off Argentina, and oil in the eastern Mediterranean.

Oil companies, logically enough, placed their first bets on waters adjacent to oil-bearing tracts of land. About 1940, American companies began drilling for oil off the coast of Texas. The Venezuelan coast came next, and then the Persian Gulf (or the Arabian Gulf, as you should call it when in conversation with Arabs). Offshore oil became recognized as the coming thing; the term – still used even when the oil is far from land – recalls that it all began with wells placed within rowing distance of the coast.

Drilling at sea, compared with drilling on land, called for the devising of a radically new technology and was bound to be more expensive. But experience soon showed that it could be profitable, and development was rapid; by now, offshore oil accounts for nearly one fifth of total production in the non-Communist world. By 1960, with the demand for oil growing fast and certain anxieties taking root about reserves under the world's land surface, oil men started thinking about possibilities farther from the coasts. In this atmosphere, international law was revised to carve up the sea,

Forties Field

which had hitherto belonged to nobody outside the traditional three-mile limit of each nation's territorial waters. A nation now enjoys jurisdiction over the sea until it reaches a depth of 200 metres, or even beyond that so far as natural resources can be exploited. Oil companies are thus protected from the possibility of making a strike in the North Sea and then finding the Russians going into business a few miles away.

The idea that there might be oil under the North Sea was not so fantastic as it may have seemed to the ordinary Englishman or Scot accustomed to associate oil with desert sands and torrid heat. There is oil in Britain, though not very much. During the last war, when petrol could be imported only at the risk of life, some oil was produced from wells in Lancashire and the Midlands. The fields were not considered rich enough to be worth working in peacetime, but the memory held its lessons. A more emphatic pointer was the discovery during the 1960s of large deposits of natural gas in the North Sea, a source of supply that has revolutionized Britain's gas industry and almost entirely replaced gas manufactured from coal. Natural gas and oil were formed, millions of years ago, by similar processes; and where you find one, you can reasonably hope to find the other.

The oil world was soon buzzing. The waters that aroused interest belonged, under the new international agreement, either to Britain or to Norway (it was soon established that the Dutch, German and Danish sectors had nothing, or only gas). The British sector has been divided into blocks measuring 100 square miles. Exploration licences were granted to approved applicants, and at one period sold off by means of an auction with sealed bids. This system encourages a strong element of hunch, not to mention luck if the block turns out to be a winner; one block went for a mere £3,200, another fetched £21 million. In the Norwegian sector all applications are negotiated and the blocks are twice as large.

All the big companies – the majors, as they call themselves – are involved: Shell, BP, Exxon, Paul Getty's Occidental, Conoco, Amoco, the French Total, the Belgian Petrofina. Because of the enormous investment required, they often go into partnership. The Brent field, which has proved to be among the richest, is owned fifty-fifty by Shell and Exxon. Consortiums are formed, too;

Forties Field

another important field, Ninian, is jointly owned by Burmah Oil, BP, Exxon, ICI and seven other companies. There is also room for 'wildcats' – small independent firms whose strength lies in their flair and ingenuity, and the quality of their geologists and technicians. To take a hand in the North Sea game, they have to find investment partners. Hamilton Brothers, a successful independent, is exploiting the Argyll field with backing from Rio Tinto Zinc, the Rothermere Press, and the merchant bank of Kleinwort Benson.

Blocks belonging to a given company or consortium are often far apart, since the policy as a rule was to take a chance here and a chance there. A map of the North Sea, now that it has been 'colonized', looks like a map of West Africa after it had been sliced up between the British, French, Portuguese and German Empires.

From photographs or from television, most people by now know the look of oil rigs and platforms – the huge structures, like science-fiction giants, that are scattered about the North

Sea. A platform (sometimes it's also called a rig, but the correct term will be used in this book for clarity) houses the production machinery when extraction of oil has begun. It can be envisaged as an artificial island, for its base is securely planted on the sea-bed hundreds of feet down. It will not rise and fall, nor will it sway in the wind, or no more than a tall building on land. The main deck stands eighty feet above water level and is about the size of Trafalgar Square. The working spaces and the crew's living quarters are housed in pre-fabricated buildings, known as modules, which are built separately and put into place after the platform is installed.

A rig is used for exploration – test-drillings to find out whether there is oil at a given spot. It moves on after a month or two, whereas a platform is designed to stay in the same place for years. In shallow waters a rig has legs which are extended hydraulically and attached to the sea-bed, but in the North Sea off Scotland this would be impracticable and the rig is held only by anchors and by having most of its weight below water level; consequently a rig does rise and fall, and pitches slightly in a strong wind, though not so much as a ship. To look at, a rig is like a platform, but generally smaller.

The oil rush begins with exploration, and this is still the main activity in the North Sea. As I write, about thirty rigs are at work in the British sector, which has been by no means exhaustively combed. Producing the oil is a far more complex operation. Between the day when a strike is made and the day when oil 'goes on flow', five years may elapse.

The first important field was discovered in 1969 by an American group headed by Phillips Petroleum, and it remains the richest in the North Sea. This field, Ekofisk, is likely to produce 30 million tons a year by 1980. It is in the Norwegian sector (although the oil is piped to Britain).

However, the British sector as a whole promises more oil than the Norwegian – a forecast that has been confidently made since major fields were discovered in 1970 and 1971, and borne out by later successes. The scoreboard so far shows nine fields with a probable output of at least 5 million tons each, as well as some smaller fields. Heading the list are three fields – Forties (BP), Brent (Shell-Exxon), and Ninian (consortium-owned) – each of which is expected to yield 20 million tons by the 1980s.

The brief history of the oil rush has been marked by one feature not expected at the outset: a movement farther and farther north. At first it was reckoned, or at least hoped, that oil would be found near to the natural gas, which lies between East Anglia and Holland. Some bright chaps hastened to buy up land in Yarmouth, the town envisaged as 'Britain's oil capital'. This title has gone, instead, to Aberdeen. But – although the exploration rigs are largely supplied from Aberdeen and nearby Peterhead, and although Aberdeen is securely established as the 'capital' because it's as far north as oil executives want to live – most of the oil is farther north still. Of the nine significant fields, only Forties is on the same latitude as Aberdeen, one other is east of the Orkneys, and the rest are east – or even north-east – of the Shetland Isles.

The size of the oil reserves is a matter for keen argument. The known fields may be richer than the companies have established (or richer than they are willing to say), more discoveries may be made in 'the patches in between', and exploration off Scotland's west coast has scarcely begun. Definitely, there is enough oil in the British sector to meet Britain's needs, while Norway can count on producing four times as much oil as she consumes. The question is, how long will it last?

Britain – except when slowed down by recession – consumes about 115 million tons of oil a year, of which 95 million tons come from the Middle East (including Libya). If all goes well, North Sea production should match British consumption by 1980 and maintain an annual rate of 150 million tons through the ensuing decade. As well as rendering us proof against Arab political pressure and possible embargoes, this ought to put our balance of payments right, for oil imports accounted for nine tenths of the £4,000 million deficit that we incurred in 1974. We might still have a trading deficit on other commodities, and we should still have to import some Middle East oil for certain purposes (not all oil is the same). But we should be able to sell quantities of oil – either in crude form or, more lucratively, as refined products – to nations such as France and Germany, perhaps to the United States.

At this production rate of 150 million tons, most analysts think that the oil will last until 2010. But according to Professor Peter Odell – who differs strongly from majority opinion, but whose estimates of North Sea gas reserves were right when everyone else was too cautious – it would last until 2040. Alternatively, if Odell's ideas about the reserves prove convincing, it would be open to Britain – if the oil companies agree – to step up production to about 300 million tons a year. By doing so we could, for a limited time, have a tremendous balance of payments surplus, always on condition that other countries buy our oil, which won't be cheaper than oil from the Middle East. This question of the rate of output may become a crucial national choice. In Norway the Government inclines strongly to keeping production at a moderate level and making the oil last as

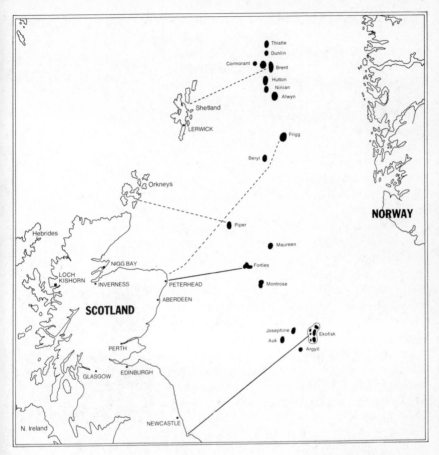

Location of the
main oil fields
and pipelines

long as possible, but of course Norway will be able in any case to sell much more than she uses. The temptation for Britain to kill the golden goose might be hard to resist, especially if we continue to lose ground in most spheres of industry and get addicted to living as a maritime Saudi Arabia.

Meanwhile, even at a production rate of 150 million tons, the Treasury will do well out of oil in terms of revenue. The oil companies will do very well too, and critics think that the Government ought to have driven a harder bargain with them, as Norway successfully did. But Norway was in a position to face the future without an oil boom, and there's all too much reason to fear that Britain is not. At all events, oil profits will be siphoned off by taxation, by a levy in the form of royalties, and (it's now envisaged) by participation between the companies and the new British National Oil Corporation. The companies are being allowed to get off lightly in the early years while they recover their investment costs, but when the oil is flowing freely the State should be getting 70% of the profits, and that could mean £2,000 million a year.

If this revenue went to an independent Scotland, it could more or less meet the budget of a nation of five million people; Scots are naturally intrigued by reading of the finances of Kuwait, where there is no income tax. Besides, Scotland could sell oil to England and have a dazzling balance of payments surplus. The oil is in Scottish waters, geographically speaking, and the idea that it is 'Scotland's oil' makes an obvious appeal. It's hardly surprising that the Scottish National Party scored triumphs in the 1974 elections, and in particular won four of the seven seats in the Grampian Region, whose centre is Aberdeen.

Below: Nigg, the largest concrete dock gate in the world

Nigg construction site

But, in these days of heavy unemployment, most people – decidedly most Scots – are more directly interested in knowing how many jobs the oil boom will bring. In this respect, the outlook is not inspiring.

More than any other major industry, oil is capital-intensive rather than labour-intensive. It provides jobs chiefly in refining, and Britain already has an adequate refining capacity, which

Japanese steel at Nigg

will work at the same rate whether the oil comes from the Middle East or the North Sea. New refineries may be built in more convenient places, namely in the north of Scotland, but even a large refinery employs hundreds of men where a steel or chemical or engineering works of comparable size and financial value would employ thousands.

There are jobs on the rigs – about 4,000 at present – but the workers come from all over Britain and Scottish unemployment is scarcely relieved; one also meets Norwegian rig-workers in the British sector, Americans in the key jobs, and Spanish cooks and cleaners. To see real opportunities for Scots, we must look to the service bases where supplies for the rigs are loaded; to construction work of various kinds; and to the manufacture of equipment.

According to official figures, the oil boom has created 14,000 jobs in Scotland, to which one should add a few thousand in north-east England. A study by Professor Gaskin of Aberdeen University raises the Scottish figure to 30,000 by taking in all kinds of contracts awarded to manufacturing firms (in some cases, a Government report tells us, the workers and even the employers don't know that they are doing anything connected with oil). But whether these workers would otherwise be doing something else or would be unemployed, it's impossible to say. At all events, it would be illusory to imagine that the oil boom is making a serious dent on Scottish unemployment, which as I write stands at 134,000. The most one can say is that unemployment might be higher than it is, for it's only marginally above the rate for Britain as a whole, and in previous recessions it has often been double.

The benefits of the oil boom are also distinctly localized. The Grampian Region, overlooking the

North Sea, has only 3.1% unemployment, half the overall rate for Scotland. Taking a closer focus, you find virtual full employment in the towns that have the service bases, while other towns along the coast have had no cause to notice that anything has happened.

Another sobering thought is that the number of jobs may never increase much, and may actually decline. Rigs consume supplies at a faster rate than the oil production platforms which will replace them, and there may never be so many platforms as there are rigs. Infrastructure projects, such as laying pipelines and building service bases, are done once and for all.

Undoubtedly there would be more jobs if British industry had seized its opportunities. The undersea pipelines have almost all been laid by American companies using Japanese steel. Building rigs demands only modest adaptability from a nation with engineering and shipbuilding traditions, but very few have been built in Britain with the shining exception of BP's Sea Quest, produced by Harland and Wolff. In 1972 Lord Balogh established that 95% of the rigs working in the North Sea had been built in the Netherlands and the rest in Germany. The next year, Norway won so many orders that she was able to rank second to the USA in rig-building; and while I was working on this book a press report brought news of twelve rigs to be built in Finland. As for supply boats, which ought to be a natural for British shipyards, the situation is better but not triumphant; eighty are under construction in Britain and a hundred elsewhere. Ironically – since all the foreign rigs, boats, steel pipes and mechanical equipment count as imports to Britain – the North Sea oil operation which is supposed to put our balance of payments into surplus has so far added £500 million a year to our deficit. And work that counts as British

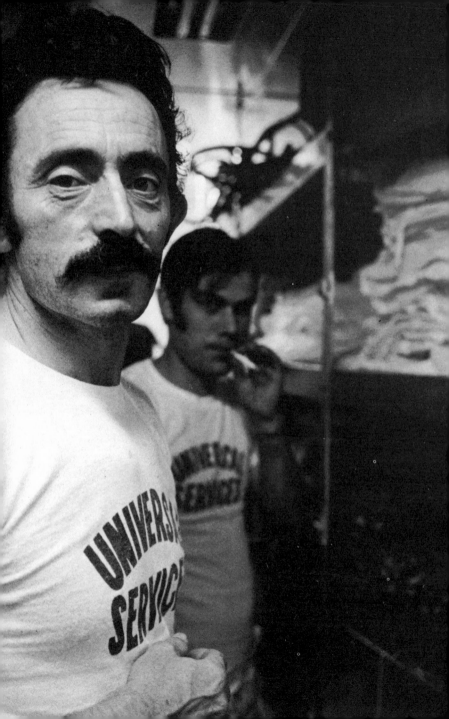

Workers on the rigs come from all over the world
Left: Spanish stewards
Above: French tool-pusher
Right: US supervisors

because it's done in Britain is often carried out with American participation or by American subsidiaries.

In 1974 the oil boom generated £1,300 million in orders of which Britain's share was £520 million, or 40%. Mr John Smith, Under-Secretary at the Department of Energy, made a statement raising this to 55% by taking account only of 'areas where British industry was able to meet orders'. These he distinguished from 'areas where the United Kingdom has little or no capabilities', which he listed as drilling rigs, undersea pipe-laying, and offshore emplacement. Just as usefully, a school might claim to teach everything except in areas where it has no capabilities, such as English, maths and history.

Since I came back from Scotland, I've often been asked whether the North Sea oil venture is going to be a success. To answer this question one would have to be a geologist, a production engineer and an economist rolled into one, and even then one could be wrong. Besides, statements about what's happening and likely to happen are generally made by oil companies, or by writers and journalists using information provided by oil companies. It is wise to receive such statements – which themselves influence events and are in a sense actions, or moves in the game – as we receive statements by politicians, rather than as the dispassionate judgements of 'experts'.

Behind the secrecy and the occasional 'disinformation', there is undoubtedly real uncertainty. The oil rush proceeds by fits and starts. Eager enthusiasm and headlong progress, spurred by competitive haste, alternate with caution and consolidation. Setbacks occur, plans are changed, financial and political calculations are revised.

This uncertainty communicates itself – for Scots are no fools – to everyone whose personal future is caught up in the oil rush. Wherever I went, I found fingers crossed. 'It could all collapse tomorrow, we realize that,' said a shop steward at a construction site. The managing director of a shipyard told me sternly that I was wasting my time by writing this book – 'the peak of the boom has passed'. In pubs, in airport lounges, in canteens, on the dockside, the refrain was the same: 'It's all right while it lasts' . . . 'There's no security' . . . 'We've had promises before.'

It's often said that the oil men expected the North Sea to be like the Gulf of Mexico. No doubt they didn't, but their methods of work could only be based on previous experience, and they have certainly met with greater difficulties than they expected. To start with, the rock-layers that hold the oil present baffling and time-consuming problems. The Jurassic strata, likely to contain the oil reservoirs, are often twisted or fractured, and are covered by other strata thicker and harder

than could be deduced from theoretical calculations, so that drilling goes slowly and drilling-bits
keep getting worn out or broken. Also, the oil
lies very deep. The accepted rule (though it may
change) is that production is uneconomic if the oil
is at a depth greater than 12,500 feet. To strike
oil and be compelled to leave it undisturbed is a
frustrating experience.

But most of the problems, and the escalating
costs, are caused by the fact that oil has been
found so far out to sea and so far to the north.
Traffic between bases and rigs or platforms is of
two kinds: crews and urgently needed portable
equipment go by helicopter, but supplies in
general go by boat. Offshore oil in the original
sense of the phrase relies on quick and easy
transport. The oilfields of the North Sea are 100
or 150 miles from land – and the land in most cases
is the Shetland Isles, to which the crews and the
supplies have to be brought in the first place.

And the North Sea, while it's shallow by
oceanic standards, is deeper than any waters in
which oil men have worked before. Worse, it gets
deeper as you go north. The semi-submersible
rig, which does not stand on the sea-bed and
depends for stability on having most of its
weight, including heavy pontoons, below the
water-line, has demanded a whole new branch of
rig-building technology. Rigs are now working
at depths of 500 feet, and at present this seems to
be about the limit. Exploration at greater depths
might be feasible, but production requires the
installation of a platform, secured to the sea-bed,
and also a fixed pipeline. Hamilton Brothers, in the
smallish Argyll field, are producing oil with a semi-
submersible rig and delivering it by tanker, which
enabled them in June 1975 to win the oil race by
making the first shipments; however, the 'majors'
insist that platforms and pipelines are necessary

in a large field. This makes it doubtful that the oil rush will extend to Scotland's Atlantic coast, where the sea is 600 feet deep or more. A senior BP executive has said: 'Whilst the capability to drill in these depths exists, that to produce does not.'

The greatest handicap is the terrible weather in the North Sea. This too gets worse as you travel north, and in the Atlantic it is worse still. Force nine winds – fifty miles an hour – can blow for days on end, especially in winter. In bad North Sea storms, gusts can reach the terrifying speed of 130 miles an hour. Storm waves can reach a height of 100 feet, compared to twenty-seven feet as a rare occurrence in the Persian Gulf. Rigs have to be built to resist a heavy battering, and there have been several disasters, mostly to rigs of a design that had proved adequate in calmer waters. Four rigs have been sunk, while others have been so badly damaged that they needed months of repair work. While on this grim note, it's worth pointing out that disasters to ships can be a serious matter in oil zones. On a dark night in August 1975, a tanker crashed into a platform in the Gulf of Mexico; five of the tanker's crew were killed and the sea was covered by a two-mile oil slick. Such an event seems more likely than not in the course of the North Sea oil boom. Once production starts, there will be a standing risk of oil

flooding into the sea, massacring fish and perhaps reaching the coast – a risk from a crash like the one just described, from a well-head explosion, or from a pipeline fracture. There are depots equipped with dispersant materials, but a study in a civil engineering journal expresses serious doubts whether they 'would be of any use at all, let alone able to deal with the sort of accident which could happen in the North Sea in the coming years'.

It is difficult and costly getting supplies and workers out to the rigs

In hard economic terms, the risk of disaster is less of a problem than the inevitable delays caused by bad weather – not only by gales but also by fogs, which are frequent in the North Sea even in summer. Helicopters are unable to land for days at a time. Rigs that have finished an exploration job can't be towed to the new location, or have to be towed very slowly. On one occasion, a rig spent sixty-five days waiting for towing to be feasible. Supply boats toss at anchor for days, even weeks, in the hope that a break in stormy weather will make

unloading possible, and sometimes have to take their cargoes back to base. In a recent winter period, it was possible to unload supplies of essential cement casing for the Forties field on only three days in each month. Dividing the winter into 360 twelve-hour periods, records showed 38 of them to be good, 49 marginal and 273 bad – which meant impossible. The good periods occur unexpectedly, when the boat may not be there, for the journey takes a day or two. It's possible to keep stocks of supplies, and crews who have finished their stint have to stay on the rig and keep working if the helicopter with the new crew doesn't arrive on time, but the total of 'down-

Aberdeen Airport after a four-hour delay through fog

Below: Aberdeen Heliport

time' – periods in which no work can be done – is about three times what it would be in familiar offshore conditions. In the winter of 1974–5, Shell's production platform was a scene of activity for only 56 days out of 183.

So exploration is slow, and getting into production is slower still. A platform takes two years to build, and it can be towed out to sea – at two miles an hour – and installed only in the brief period of good summer weather. Thus, a platform due for completion in May which doesn't get built until August is for practical purposes a year late; and this has happened. Meanwhile, the pipeline has to be laid. The Forties pipeline, now complete, runs 110 miles under the sea to Cruden Bay, near Aberdeen, and then a similar distance underground to the refinery at Grangemouth on the Firth of Forth. Laying the pipeline also takes two years and doesn't always meet the time-table; recently a pipeline snapped and months of work were wasted. It is almost predictable that, when the target date for production arrives, either the platform will be waiting for the pipeline or the other way round. Moreover, the complex production process requires a variety of equipment – engines, pumps, pressure-gauges, to name only a few items – which may be delayed by changes in specification, by poor management or by strikes. For want of a nail the battle may be lost, or victory at least deferred.

When the existence of major oilfields was confirmed, it was expected that Britain would get a symbolic trickle in 1974 and that the first year of significant production – 25 million tons – would be 1975. In the event, 1974 is 1975 and 1975 will be 1976. The wonder is that the time-table is only a year behind.

The costs of the oil boom are enormous; they have risen almost Concorde-fashion since the ori-

Left: Gas pipelines being laid near Peterhead
Below: Shell's pipeline comes ashore at Firth Voe in the Shetlands, later to be dropped underground to the terminal at Sullom Voe. BP's pipeline coming ashore at Cruden Bay is completely camouflaged. The picture (above left opposite) shows reception facilities and relief tanks set well back from the shore

Right, below: The
salmon fishermen work
on undisturbed at
Cruden Bay – 'so long as
the pipe doesn't fracture'

ginal estimates, partly because of inflation but
mainly because the mounting difficulties have
made new technical developments necessary;
and they are still rising. A semi-submersible rig
costs about £12 million to build and £30,000 a day
to operate. A platform costs anything from £20
million to £60 million. Establishing a well-head
costs at least £1,500,000, in some cases £3 million,
and a field will have twenty or thirty wells, depending on its shape. Undersea pipeline costs £700,000
a mile. All these expenses are incurred before the
first gallon of oil comes out of the rock. Investment figures were reckoned at the outset to be
£1,200 for each barrel of production per day (peak
production from a major field should be 400,000

barrels a day) but they now stand at £3,000. The
capital so far invested in North Sea oil is put at
£1,000 million, and by the time full production is
reached in 1980 it will probably be £5,000 million.
Another estimate makes it £8,000 million – we are
in the realm of guesswork.

An executive in an American company gave me
a graphic comparison between costs in the Middle
East and costs in the North Sea. On land, he said,
production costs are between ten and twenty cents
a barrel; in the North Sea they are from two to four
dollars, without counting such extras as undersea
pipelines. Now, until 1973 the world price of
oil was $4 a barrel, which gives us an insight into
the profits being made. The Arabs and the other
exporting nations have raised the price to $12 –
very luckily for anyone banking on North Sea
prospects. You may ask why the oil companies
took any interest in the North Sea before 1973,
when their costs could be as high as the selling
price then in force. A BP document answers:
'Firstly, it is near one of the world's four main
industrial markets; secondly, the political attitudes
of the countries bordering and controlling it
appear – at least at present – to be stable.' One
might add (thirdly, frankly and I should think
most importantly) that when they made the decision the companies didn't expect their costs to be
anything like what they have become.

Hence the uncertainties. But four other factors
have to be taken into account. One: we are in a
world recession and the demand for oil, closely
related to industrial activity, is static after over a
century of rising at dizzy speed. Two: the world
price could fall because of this recession, as well
as because of decisions by Arabs and others, and
possible profits from the North Sea would fall
correspondingly. Three: oil companies, wealthy
as they are, borrow from banks when engaged in

Forties Field

major operations. Interest rates are high and must be added to other preliminary expenses; more significantly, the willingness of the banks to lend depends on their estimates of future profits, and there are distinct signs of a cash flow problem. Four: the oil companies object strongly to the British Government's taxation plans, which they see as imperilling a 'reasonable' return on their investment.

Oil men would not be oil men (or good poker-players, which most of them are too) if it didn't occur to them that the Government might have fresh and milder thoughts about taxation if the oil rush looked like slowing down – or, in the extreme case, grinding to a halt. What would happen, for instance, if production from the British sector didn't meet Britain's needs until 1982 instead of 1980? The British economy, after all, is hanging on by its finger-nails and buying 'international confidence' with the promise of restoring the balance of payments, and time is not on our side.

Part of my reading before I went to view the North Sea scene was an informative article in the *Sunday Times Business News*. I learned from it that American oil companies have demoted the North Sea from top to fourth place in their list of 'attractive prospects', below the US itself, Nigeria and Indonesia (where it's possible to pay no tax at all, other than bribes). Considering the uncertainties in the North Sea, the article said, they would regard 25% as a minimum rate of return on investment; but Ninian, to name one big field, looks like earning only 19%. If things are like this, I read with growing fascination, 'some companies would be strongly tempted to leave their oil beneath the sea'. These hints were underlined by one hard fact: Conoco, developer of the Hutton field with a potential output of ten million tons a year, 'is halting £20 million of work until the

Hamilton's
Transworld 58 rig

Government stance becomes clearer'.

When I found myself visiting a rig working for Conoco, the company attitude was expounded to me by the supervisor, Jim Dunlap. I had the impression that he was encouraged to enlighten visitors, but he is a forthright Texan too and if he was carrying out a task, he did it with conviction. How long, I asked innocently, did he expect the oil boom to last? 'Well, that depends on your Government. So long as it can't decide on the terms to offer the companies, and so long as it pulls these ridiculous taxes, we don't know where we stand. You get some lunatic like this Wedgwood Benn interfering, our work becomes impossible.' I pointed out that the Government had announced its terms (as a matter of fact, they were announced by Mr Benn's predecessor at the Department of Energy). 'Maybe,' said Mr Dunlap, 'but you know how things happen, you have another election and it's all changed.' Soon afterwards, Mrs Thatcher visited Aberdeen and announced that the terms would indeed be revised

under a Conservative Government.

Despite the huge investment, despite the confident forecasts, despite the glowing optimism voiced by the Prime Minister and many others, the North Sea oil boom remains a gamble. But it is a gamble on which thousands of working men are staking their livelihoods – and some their lives.

Forties Field at night, still a hive of activity

ON THE RIGS

As we come in by helicopter, the rig looks like a Meccano toy for a giant. Half a mile away the stand-by boat pitches among the grey waves; it is there to warn off fishing trawlers or other shipping when visibility is bad, and also to rescue any rig-workers who may happen to be blown into the sea. Otherwise, there's nothing but an expanse of rolling, dangerous-looking water.

The derrick, a tapering tower of steel, rises ninety feet above the drilling-floor, and the derrick-man in his cabin is about halfway up. There are three decks. The top one, open to the winds, has nothing much except the landing-pad for the helicopter. The second deck is the drilling-floor, where the vital operations are carried on. The lower deck, much the largest, is storage space and is stacked with the lengths of steel that are used voraciously in drilling work. In the middle of the

Conoco's Pentagone 82 drilling rig

Conoco's Pentagone 82
drilling rig

rig, rather alarmingly, there's a cavity and you peer straight down to the sea; this is known as the moon-pool. Doors lead to the operations rooms and the living quarters. Inside, it's much like being on a ship – long corridors, sharp corners, flights of steel steps.

Some rigs are owned by oil companies, notably Shell and BP, but in most cases they belong to drilling companies and are hired by the oil companies for varying periods. This is, in particular, the American system. The oil world is a jigsaw of contracts and sub-contracts; on the same rig you'll find employees of the oil company, the drilling company, a geological company, a catering company, and one or more companies doing repair and maintenance work.

Names for the different jobs are taken from American usage and are distinctly picturesque. The men on the lower deck are the roustabouts; they are general labourers, mostly employed to get the materials unloaded from the supply boats and moved up to the drilling-floor when needed. On the drilling-floor, where the work is rather more skilled, the men are known as roughnecks. The key man is the tool-pusher – he pushes the tools along, keeps the rhythm of work going, and decides (in consultation with the supervisor from the oil company) when drilling is to start or stop. The driller, who presses the buttons and watches the sea-bed on a television screen, also has a responsible job, and the derrick-man is important too. Then there are crane-drivers, mechanics, and geologists who examine the samples brought up by the drilling.

There are no fixed grades of labourers and craftsmen, as in a British factory. The promotion ladder is from roustabout to roughneck, then to driller or derrick-man, ultimately to tool-pusher – although roustabouts aren't always keen to become

Above and opposite: Conoco rig

roughnecks because it's considered more dangerous. A few companies have training schemes, but as a rule you learn a job when you have to do it. Tool-pushers have complete authority in transferring men from one job to another when accident or illness creates a need. Some men complain of being suddenly ordered to do tricky work on the drilling-floor which they may never have even watched. Some complain, on the other hand, that they can't get jobs for which they are qualified by previous experience in industry. 'It all goes by whether your face fits,' I was told repeatedly.

Tool-pushers and other men in senior jobs are usually Americans or Canadians. The drilling company is likely to be American, and it was along

Drilling engineer

Mud technician

the Texas coast that the technique of offshore drilling was developed. However, a roughneck who has worked in the North Sea for five years feels resentful when he has to take orders from a tool-pusher straight from the USA, whose experience has been in smaller rigs and easier conditions. A feeling has developed that Americans have the top jobs by right of nationality. A trade union official in Aberdeen said to me reflectively: 'Well, in the old days an Englishman would be sent out to give the orders on the Indian railways, and an Indian couldn't get above a certain level if he stayed on the job all his life. Now we're finding out what that feels like.' Americans in the oil industry argue that, when an Englishman or a Scot is qualified for a higher job, he'll go abroad to escape British income tax. Americans working in the North Sea, of course, pay tax at US rates.

Work on the rigs goes on round the clock, except for 'down-time', with two shifts. Everyone works twelve hours a day (or night) seven days a week. As one man said to me grimly: 'You're filthy, you're wet, you're freezing, and you know you've got to carry on for twelve hours.' It is forbidden to go indoors during the shift; the men get one meal after six hours, eaten in a little hut on the deck, and the next meal in the canteen after coming off work. If a man is needed, he has to work even beyond this 84-hour week. A crane-driver told me: 'I've known what it is to work twelve hours, get three hours' sleep, and be woken up to start again.'

Over the year, a crew is on the rig half the time and on leave half the time. The usual system is a fortnight on and a fortnight off; on some rigs it's only a week, on some as much as four weeks. A Canadian supervisor told me with emphasis that there ought to be a law against making the stint more than two weeks – 'the men get tense, you get quarrels starting.' But if the helicopter with the relief crew is delayed by bad weather, the men simply have to carry on. I heard of men who had been on a rig for six weeks.

We arrive in Aberdeen with permission to visit two rigs, one working for Conoco and the other for Hamilton Brothers. The Hamilton rig, Transworld 58, is particularly interesting – indeed unique – because it isn't test-drilling but extracting oil. As well as the stand-by boat, a big tanker waits nearby. Sadly, the weather plays us false. The wind is blowing at fifty miles an hour, the white-caps on the waves evoke uneasy thoughts, and the

Result of fog at Aberdeen Airport

helicopter pilot says he won't shut down his engines and we can't stay more than twenty minutes. Helicopters don't fly in conditions worse than this; a roughneck hurries up to me and gives me a letter to post. We make a speedy tour of Transworld 58. It looks impressive, with silver-painted pipes and tanks everywhere, more like a refinery than a drilling-rig. Then we fly back to Aberdeen. The 180-mile journey, which had taken an hour and a half, takes two and a quarter hours on the return trip in the teeth of the wind.

The Conoco rig is off the Shetlands, so we have an unexpected chance to visit these distant islands. The rig is called Pentagone 82; I grasp that this is because it has five legs instead of the usual four, and wonder vaguely why the word is spelt with a final 'e'. The reason is that it's operated by a French company, Forax-Neptune; it was built in Brownsville, Texas, to a French design. About half the workers are French and half British. The latter predominate among the humble roustabouts. We wait at Aberdeen airport for the arrival of a Caravelle from Paris. When we board the Conoco charter plane for Sumburgh, the Shetland airport, it's full of lively French conversation. I gather that in Paris there's *une chaleur incroyable*. But at

Lounge on Conoco rig four hours after expected departure by helicopter. These men later missed their connection and were stranded in makeshift accommodation for two nights in Shetland

Sumburgh it's chilly, and after transferring to the
helicopter we fly through mist and drizzle. It
isn't windy by North Sea standards, but as I go
along the walkways on the outer edge of the decks
I hold tight to the rail.

It's mid-afternoon, so we have a meal with
Pierre Cordey, the rig manager, and Jim Dunlap,
the Conoco supervisor. They seem to rank as
equals, and the same is true of the two cooks, one
French and one English. All rig-workers I've
talked to, whatever their other complaints, agree
that the food on the rigs is excellent. We look
at the living-quarters. Each room has two upper
and two lower bunks; of course, because of the
shift system, only two men will be sleeping
in it at a time. It's the size of an average hotel
room, with a shower and good cupboard space.
The recreation room isn't crowded, although there
are eighty men on the rig and only forty are
working at present. Perhaps it fills up for the
evening film show. A notice says: 'The use of
ashtrays is a sign of well education,' and the same
in French. Smoking is allowed only in off-duty
space and off-duty time. Naturally, alcohol is
forbidden on rigs.

We go out to the drilling-floor. The shaft is
whizzing round and round, on the same principle
as a carpenter's electric drill, as the bit eats its way
into rocks eleven thousand feet down. After
twelve hours, more or less, the bit will wear out
and will have to be changed, which takes ten
hours. This is an inevitable part of the process and
doesn't count as down-time. Much more frequently
– whenever the drill goes down thirty feet –
another length of steel has to be inserted. This is
called 'making a connection' and is the main task of
the roughnecks. And as the drill goes down, a
cement casing is forced into the rock to make the
hole keep its shape, so that the drill can go down

again after the bit is changed. The hole has a dia-meter of 36 feet just below the sea-bed, narrowing to 17 feet deep down. Dunlap explains that it's possible to drill in very rough weather, but not possible to change the bit, bring up samples for testing, or run in the casing. He says that Penta-gone 82 carries enough supplies to carry on for ten days if boats don't arrive or can't unload. Down-time averages about 15%, mostly caused by difficulties in moving the rig to a new location.

After a while, three roughnecks get into position to make a connection. The shaft has to be caught in two big steel clamps which bite viciously as the roughnecks hold them steady. It is unscrewed, it swings aside, the new length of steel piping is fitted into place, and finally the hovering shaft is brought back again. The job calls for physical strength, real skill, and split-second timing. If you get your hand in the way of the clamp or your head in the way of the loose length of piping . . . if you slip or stumble or move too slowly . . . you're in trouble. The drilling-floor has walls and parts of it are covered by metal roofing, but round the shaft it's open to the sky. We are seeing the connection made in easy conditions. It might be raining, and the steel floor would be slippery. The rig might be rising and falling. It might be dark, and in winter it usually is; the drilling-floor has powerful floodlights but roughnecks say that the derrick casts deceptive shadows. Dunlap guesses at my thoughts and says quickly: 'We don't get any accidents. These guys know their job.' However, one of the three is very young and it's obvious that he is learning.

I go down to the lower deck. The stairway, in fact a steel ladder, is steeply pitched and I shouldn't care to negotiate it in a storm. It's a long way and I'm glad to arrive. The deck is covered with heavy wooden containers and with stacks of steel

Conoco rig

Making a connection

piping. I find myself at the bow, rather to my surprise as the rig is practically square. Pentagone 82 has three engines and can move under its own power, but this is done only for 'parking' and normally it's towed by two supply-boats.

Then I have a look at one of the legs. They go down 140 feet to the pontoons, which need maintenance or repairs from time to time. A man has to climb down a vertical ladder inside the leg. Some of the newest rigs have lifts, I'm told.

After this, I see the mud-room. Mud is vital in drilling; it is pumped down as far as the drill goes, and serves to keep the pressure inside the shaft higher than in the surrounding water. Despite the rather contemptuous name, it isn't just any old mud, but a chemical mixed to a scientific formula. The raw material is brought by the supply-boats; it is made up in four big hoppers, and three huge noisy pumps do the rest of the job. The mud circulates, and when it comes up again it brings the 'cuttings' – fragments of the rock that has lain undisturbed for 300 million years. This is the object of the whole operation. The mud, with its cuttings, is delivered to a tray, where it looks like sodden clay with a scattering of stones – to the ignorant eye, very much what you'd get by digging your garden on a wet day. The cuttings go to a room where they are noted by two 'mud-loggers', and where a geologist examines them with a microscope and a fluoroscope. Final evaluation of the best cuttings will be made in a laboratory, so they are kept in little envelopes and put away in box-files. This corner of the room could be the correspondence-filing section of any office, or the cuttings file (in another sense) of a newspaper library. It seems a slight reward for all this arduous work and for an expense of £30,000 a day. And it takes an effort of the imagination to realise that these little brown envelopes may govern our

140 feet down to
pontoons

country's economic future.

The rig has been on this spot for thirty-seven days, and will be moving on in another eight days, having completed its test-drilling in record time thanks to the fine summer. I find myself anxious to know whether there's oil here. Apparently there is, but the company has yet to decide whether the quality and quantity make it commercial.

There are certain jobs for which, if one has any capacity for sympathy, no reward could be too high. Having been down coal-mines, I see no objection at all to paying miners £100 a week, since I know that I wouldn't take the job for £200. I now feel the same about rig-workers, and I wish it were true – as most people seem to believe – that they are earning colossal wages. In fact, although high wages are being paid in certain spheres of the oil rush, these are earned on land, at the supply bases and the construction sites. The men on the

rigs earn less. This is primarily because the companies don't recognize trade unions or any form of wage bargaining. Another reason is that the workers in the supply bases are mostly local men, in towns with full or almost full employment, whereas the rig-workers are recruited from all over Britain – from the reserve army of the unemployed.

Wages vary from company to company, and have risen over the years. They were very poor indeed when the rigs first appeared in the North Sea; it seems that they have quadrupled since the late 1960s, which means that they've roughly doubled in relation to the average national wage or to the cost of living. Roustabouts – who are the majority of the labour-force – earn £120 to £130 a week, roughnecks £140 to £150, and catering workers about £80. The flat rate over the long working week puts them at a disadvantage. Under a normal union agreement, they would be getting overtime beyond forty hours a week, double time at weekends, extra rates for working in unpleasant and dangerous conditions, and probably bonus money. (Some drilling companies pay a lump-sum bonus after six months in order to reduce turnover, but most do not.) Union officials say that in most industries a man who worked 84 hours a week would earn more than the rig-workers. One rig-worker told me that he'd been better off gutting fish in the Aberdeen market; but fishing is in the doldrums now, so he's on the rigs.

Seen as an annual income, the rig-worker's pay must be halved because he works two weeks on and two weeks off. A few companies pay a retainer for time ashore, but most pay nothing. By comparison, a factory worker is earning steadily for 49 weeks in the year and drawing his basic pay for three weeks' holiday, while a merchant seaman – with a job pretty much like a rig-worker's – is

Left: Mud room
Below: Mud cuttings files

entitled to twelve weeks of paid shore leave in the year. During his 'resting' weeks, the rig-worker is in reality unemployed, but isn't allowed to draw unemployment benefit because he is not available to take another job. He may be more indisputably unemployed in winter, when some rigs cease work – but in the winter of 1975–76 he'd have been lucky to find a job.

If the rig-worker has a wife and family, he naturally has expenses such as rent which must be met throughout the year; his free food while at work doesn't weigh heavily in the total budget. If he's single and has no settled home, he has to find lodgings in Aberdeen, which are far from cheap. After the strain and isolation of life on the rig, a man coming back to civilisation with £240 for his fortnight's work in his wallet is likely to see it dwindle fast in a few days of drinking and taking out girls. One roustabout, who came from Bristol, told me that he couldn't afford to go back there and he would be paying £32 for his fortnight's bed and breakfast in Aberdeen. Some companies pay fares (including Forax-Neptune for its French as well as its British workers) but most of them don't. If a company chooses to be mean, the worker has no redress. For instance, pay is reckoned to begin when he reaches the rig. If he's told to report for work on a certain day and finds that he can't get to the rig – perhaps because the helicopter is grounded by bad weather, perhaps because the seats have been given to visiting executives or to contractors' men going out to do repair work – he may be stranded without money and without accommodation.

Then, any rig-worker has a measurable chance that sooner or later he'll be off work because of injury. He has no guarantee of getting his job back, especially if he is considered to have been careless; he gets no pay while he recovers; and he's

Below: Rig-workers' pub, Aberdeen

Just back from Stavanger, Norway, American construction workers await further work in an Aberdeen b&b hotel. 'The money on Shell's Condeep (platform) was *fantastic,* but we didn't save any'

Right: Five minutes before opening time outside rig-workers' pub, Aberdeen

unlikely to get any compensation, since he has no union to take up his case and very little hope of proving negligence on the part of the company. In American eyes, he's lucky to be getting free National Health Service treatment.

Safety on the rigs has improved considerably since the early days. (So have conditions in various other respects, such as the provision of good waterproof clothing.) At the outset, the companies took the stand that they didn't have to conform to British law on industrial safety or compensation, since they were working on the high seas. They have abandoned this claim, and the Health and Safety Act – which came into force on 1 January 1975 – has been a notable landmark. It lays down stringent standards and provides for inspectors to visit the rigs. There are not enough inspectors

Sunday afternoon in Aberdeen b&b. Geoff (right) lost a finger offshore in Portugal, lost two months' wages, no compensation, and lost bonus for making claim. Lives in Brighton – cheaper than drinking in Aberdeen. Barry (left), 17, has been on the rigs for three months. Couldn't get a job at home in Devon

Sandy from Oban, enjoys work on a platform – 'though none of the lifeboats is in the right place, and there are 309 men where there is only space for 90'

and few visits have yet been made, but rig-workers have noticed that things have changed. Stairways have been rebuilt at a more gradual angle, walkways across the moon-pool have been widened, rails have appeared where there were no rails before.

Still, the work will always be dangerous. Supplies often have to be unloaded in rough weather; the seamen on the supply-boats get the worst of it, often working up to their waists in water, but the roustabouts too have to keep their footing, watch for sudden high waves, and keep an eye on the crane swinging its load of steel pipes, all at the same time. Being swept into the sea, or blown into the sea, is the rig-worker's nightmare. In winter, with the water temperature at four degrees centigrade, survival time is put at a maximum of five minutes. The roughnecks work higher up, but jobs like 'making a connection' place them at constant risk.

A crane-driver says: 'I remember working a leaky crane – there was oil all over the deck. I reported it, but they didn't care. The supplies had to be unloaded. Of course a bloke slipped and broke his ribs. Things are better now, but you never get a spell without accidents. On my last trip, a roughneck was hit in the face by a flying bolt and a driller lost two fingers when a cement casing fell apart.'

A man sitting beside me on the plane to the Shetlands: 'I've been on the rigs for four years. Myself, I've lost two teeth and had a broken ankle. I've only seen one man killed – that was a crane-driver, the load fell and crushed his cab. They had to burn through the metal to get him out. But I've heard of plenty of other accidents, of course. There was one crane that worked loose and crashed into the sea. The man never had a chance.'

A man on his way home from a Shell rig: 'In

John, Texan rigger foreman in Forties Field, works 100–125 hours a week and earns 'fantastic' money on contract. 'It's the only way I could figure to buy a ranch and retire at 40.' First visit to shore in three months because of injured shoulder. Safety on board derrick barges 'excellent'

nineteen months, that's the time I've been on the rig, I've lost two good friends. Both swept over the side and drowned. I've seen two chaps take nasty falls and break their legs. Crushed fingers, cuts streaming with blood, men knocked out with a crack on the head – that kind of thing's normal, it's part of the life.'

A letter in the press: 'Last year I worked as a painter on an oil rig. . . . While I was on board there were several accidents: one man lost two fingers, another was knocked unconscious for two days by a drill pipe, another broke a leg, another fell in the water, was in for seven minutes and his legs were numb. That was in summer.'

Drilling companies have a reputation for callousness. Work doesn't stop when a man is killed; this is shocking to many British workers. In the mining industry, for example, it's an established tradition to close the pit for the day after a death. What is certain is that they don't spend much on medical attention. Each rig has 'medics', but they are simply workers who have studied a first-aid handbook, and may or may not hold a certificate. When an accident happens they'll be at work, probably with filthy hands; sometimes they are catering workers and will be down in the living-quarters, far from the deck which is the scene of danger. A large rig may have well over a hundred men aboard, and a merchant ship with a crew of that size would have a doctor. Nurses on the rigs (male or female) ought surely to be a requirement. An injured man is taken ashore by helicopter, but the flight both ways – assuming that the weather is good enough – takes four hours, plus the ambulance journey from airport to hospital, a distance of eight miles in Aberdeen and twenty-six miles in the Shetlands. A recent report by a group of Scottish doctors suggests helicopter pads at these hospitals, and also the formation of

teams of doctors and surgeons ready to fly to oil rigs in emergencies. After years of drilling work in the North Sea, it's strange indeed that these proposals haven't been made before.

According to this report, the chances of being killed on an oil rig are twice as great as on a fishing trawler. This is remarkable, because trawlers actually sink or catch fire at sea; only four rigs have sunk, and in three cases the whole crew was rescued. Thus, the dangers on the rigs arise from continual accidents, not from disasters affecting groups of men. The chances of death, the report also says, are ten times as great as in coal-mining and fifty times as great as in industry as a whole. I had, before reading this, done my own arithmetic, and I make the rigs to be twenty times as dangerous as the mines. The fact is that there's no

Above: Cargo is 'snatched' onto platform from supply boat, which is not tied up

Left and right: Supply boat tied up to derrick barge. Here a man was just starting to cross when the wooden plank shattered. The rigger foreman was Texas John (see previous page)

Supply boat unloading in the Forties Field

62

single authority responsible for keeping figures of deaths and injuries in the North Sea. The doctors' report uses a figure of nine deaths in 1974, but another source – a parliamentary reply by the Department of Energy – gives the figure as twelve.

The Department also informed the House of Commons that in 1974 there were 25 serious and 412 minor accidents. When quoted to experienced rig-workers, these figures are received with bitter laughter. It's up to the company, of course, to classify an injury as serious or not. A rig-worker said to me: 'I could introduce you to a man who got a fractured tibia and three broken ribs, and that was listed as bruises. He wasn't flown ashore till the next day, when the helicopter was due to come anyway.' As for genuinely minor accidents, most of them are never recorded at all. The figure of 412, this man reckoned, might be correct for two or three rigs out of the thirty in the North Sea.

The reader must be wondering by this time why anyone sticks the life on the rigs. Some men don't, of course. A man who himself finds it congenial and intends to stay said: 'You get some of them asking to be taken off by the next flight, and lots more who just finish their fortnight for the money and quit. Once a man's on the rig he can see what the risks are, obviously.' The turnover is naturally large. An elderly railwayman in Aberdeen said that he'd seen dozens of men go off to the rigs, but most of them were back on the railways. The fact remains that, among the rig-workers I've talked to, the majority said that they were going to stay.

I rather expected to find that rig-workers were a special breed of men – adventurous, buccaneering, seekers after new experience, men with no strong roots anywhere. But if I'd been meeting

Sumburgh Airport, Shetland

them in the bus queue outside the Ford factory at Dagenham, instead of at airports and in helicopters, they would have seemed to me a cross-section of the British working-class: some talkative and others reserved, some quite well and others badly educated, of all ages up to about forty, many with families. 'What does your wife think of your doing this work?' was the one question that worried them. 'Obviously no woman agrees with it,' said a man from the Midlands. 'She's got to realise it's better for me, that's all.'

However, the average man doesn't choose to do eighty-four hours a week of exhausting work, far from his home and family. Nor, for that matter, does the average man want to be idle for frequent fortnights, especially in winter. Quite a number of rig-workers have worked away from home on construction projects, or have been in the regular Army or Navy, or have been merchant seamen. I met one who had spent years at sea, once on an Antarctic whaler which didn't enter a port for twenty-two months; it suited him, evidently. All of these, nevertheless, formed a minority among the men with an ordinary working-class background.

'Our lads are no' so daft as to go out to the rigs,' a man in Peterhead said dourly. And if you live on the oil coast itself, where you can earn good money at a supply base and stay at home, you're likely to make that choice. Scots are represented on the rigs no more heavily than in Britain's population as a whole, and most of them come from the central industrial belt. Unemployment is an obvious recruiting-sergeant for the rigs. Here is a job in which you serve no apprenticeship, the employer doesn't ask about your record or qualifications, and everyone is paid the same and has the same chance of promotion.

For some, there is the challenge and pride of

Opposite page, top:
Aberdeen Heliport

Above left, left and
opposite below:
Sumburgh Airport

'the toughest job in the world'. One man said: 'It's hard work, that's true. But I've never minded that and I like an outdoor job – it keeps you fit.' For some, the attraction is found in the self-contained atmosphere, the close friendships, the world of what sociologists call 'male bonding'. 'The food's good, we're all mates together, it's sort of cosy. Mind you, I'm in the engine-room.' Some enjoy the alternation of intensive work and complete leisure – 'it's a nice life-style.' A man from the south of England said: 'No, Scotch blokes don't go in for it, they'd want more money. The money's not all that great, see, but what I like is the two weeks off. I've got some friends coming up and we're going to tour the Highlands. Another time I'll stay in Aberdeen, another time I'll go to London. It's variety.'

Another phrase kept cropping up: 'There's no hassle.' It could be said that there's hassle all the time – you can be switched to a different team, or made to do unfamiliar work, at the whim of the tool-pusher. But there are no fixed rules about how to work and where to work, no arguments about piece-rates, and no trade unions or shop

Four hours' wait, Aberdeen Airport

Sumburgh Airport

stewards to lay down that an individual is breaching conventions or agreements by working at a faster pace or taking a greater risk. 'You know where you stand,' it's also said. There is a single authority, arbitrary but positive, and an absence of pedantic dispute or complex regulation.

In Scotland, people with democratic and freedom-loving principles see the oil companies as antagonists. The American manager or supervisor is a clear embodiment of the powerful forces behind him. He is almost always a Southerner, he is politically an extreme conservative, he doesn't propose to adopt local habits or sympathise with local traditions in Aberdeen any more than in Dhahran, he believes emphatically in 'the work ethic and not the welfare ethic' (as Richard Nixon was fond of saying), and he doesn't hide his opinion that the British don't work hard enough. He is the monarch of his rig. One roughneck described to me how a tool-pusher came into the canteen and said to a man just starting on his dinner: 'That's my seat, boy.' The man pointed out that the canteen was full and he wasn't aware of any reserved places; next day he was on the outgoing helicopter. I heard, too, of men being sacked for objecting to overtime work beyond the 84-hour week. The system is: 'If you don't like it, get off.'

However, there is very little primitive 'anti-Yank' feeling in Scotland. Scots generally prefer the men from Texas, even as opponents, to devious and effete upper-class Englishmen. Left-wingers and militant trade unionists regard the authoritarian tool-pusher simply as the champion of a particularly ruthless form of capitalism, and are almost glad to find the stereotype so real. What they say is that the authoritarian method of management must be changed.

The difficulty – not on the onshore establish-

Below: On the way to
Conoco rig

On the way out
to Hamilton rig

ments and construction sites, but on the rigs – is that many of the workers take kindly to it. They often come from the south of England, where trade unionism is weak; in one small group I met men from Southampton, Portsmouth and Brighton. They know that they're working very hard and they could be better paid, but they don't find this outrageous – 'you know what it's like when you sign on, so why grumble afterwards?' A man who had tried hard to recruit trade union members said to me angrily: 'They're fatalistic. They're like zombies.' Doubtless there was a good deal of truth in his claim that the workers on his rig were too frightened to stand up for their rights – frightened of never being promoted, frightened of being picked on for the most unpleasant work, frightened of getting the sack and going home to join the unemployed. It's also true, however, that there are rig-workers who see trade unionism, rather than the oil company, as a form of authority from which they choose to escape. 'No, nobody on this rig wants the unions to come in,' said a Forax-Neptune man. 'Union blokes don't want to work, they just talk and start strikes.' And a man from a Shell rig, when I asked why he had come to the North Sea from his native Birmingham, said: 'Because there's no bloody unions, that's why. They're always making you go on strike whether you want to or not. Back home I was always either on strike or on the dole.'

Naturally, the companies encourage these attitudes. On a rig belonging to Odeco, I was told, newspaper articles attacking unions and 'militants' are pinned to the notice-board in the recreation room. Jim Dunlap, the Conoco supervisor, said to me: 'Everybody's happy here, there's never any tension or quarrels, and it'll be like that unless the unions get in and start giving orders about who can do what. The companies have just leaned over backwards to keep the men happy in order to keep the unions out.'

The unions in Aberdeen have formed a joint committee to organize the rigs. It isn't an easy task, not merely because of the prejudices I've mentioned, but also because rig-workers come

Aberdeen rig-workers' pub

Aberdeen rig-workers' pub

from all over Britain and tend to disperse when they get out of the helicopter. Only one company, on a single occasion, has allowed a trade union representative to visit a rig. Generally, the companies say that they will be delighted to agree to recognition when the unions have recruited 50% of the workers. The unions now claim to have reached this figure on the Shell and BP rigs, and it seems likely (as I write) that the companies will agree to a ballot.

In May 1975 a crane-driver named Norman Gardiner was sacked from the Ocean Victory, an Odeco rig working for Occidental Oil. He had made a mistake in operating his crane, but it was a mistake often made before and there seems no doubt that he was dismissed because he was an active trade unionist; the men had elected him as shop steward, though the position wasn't recognized by the company. The unions declared a boycott of the Odeco rigs – Odeco is one of the major drilling companies – and they were thus deprived of supplies, not only from Britain but

from anywhere in Europe because the boycott was endorsed by the International Transport Federation. As a result, Gardiner was reinstated. When I talked to him, he said that the battle had been won because of the boycott, not because he had the support of the men on the Ocean Victory. 'They do support me, mind, they want to have shop stewards, but if the company could get away with sacking a few the rest would get scared.' The supervisor had told him frankly: 'There are four men we want to get rid of, but now we can't.' By painstaking efforts, Gardiner has built up union membership on his rig to twenty-seven out of sixty men on board. He was counting on passing the 50% mark soon, but wasn't sure that the company would sign agreements even then.

It is a slow process. Men like Gardiner must wish that they were Norwegians. Under Norwegian law, the companies can recruit labour only through the trade unions, and all rig crews in the Norwegian sector have been union members right from the start, with the right to collective bargaining and protection from unjustified dismissal; nor have I heard that these rigs are at all unhappy.

National Union of Seamen's office, Aberdeen

DIVERS ARE SPECIAL

Among the thousands of men caught up in the oil rush, divers are the elite. They stay at certain hotels and boarding-houses in Aberdeen, drink in certain bars, and mostly know one another. They're employed by diving companies which also provide their equipment (another contract) and two companies, Comex and Oceaneering, dominate this aspect of the North Sea scene. There is a serious shortage of divers, especially good experienced divers. So far they have worked mainly from the rigs, making investigations and doing repairs at the drilling-point; but they're also needed on the undersea pipelines, and when platforms are installed there will be an increasing demand for divers to tend the well-heads. As a diving superintendent, who has retired from diving himself, said to me: 'They're screaming out for divers.' Divers work in pairs, and as a rule there are six on a rig. Since exploration began in the North Sea, the number of divers has risen from two hundred to almost a thousand.

At the outset, most of the divers had been in the Navy and had therefore been given a thorough training. Now the job is attracting men without previous experience – men who, at best, have done some scuba-diving as a sport. The profession isn't immune from the North Sea system of 'learn as you go along'. A diver whom I met on Pentagone 82 said that he thought training was pointless. He had worked for three years for a salvage company, diving in shallow coastal waters, and then felt confident enough to go down in the North Sea,

where he has to work at a depth of 500 feet. Comex has a training-school, but the demands from the rigs are so insistent that there is pressure to send out an untrained or partly trained diver. Now, a Government school has been opened. The divers I met took the view that it would be a non-starter because the salary for instructors will be only £5,000 a year, and an experienced diver can earn more than that either by diving or, if he's had enough, as superintendent on a rig.

The diver goes down in a bell, gets out, and does his work – with a hammer or a spanner or whatever he needs. 'We're just under-water labourers,' one diver remarked modestly. The pressure from deep water builds up concentrations of gases in his blood-stream, and despite the air reaching him through his breathing-pipe he is functioning under abnormal conditions, which carry a risk of exhaustion and therefore of accidents caused by inattention. At a depth of more than 200 feet it isn't advisable for a diver to work for longer than an hour. When he comes up, he has to enter a decompression chamber where his body is gradually restored to normal. The decompression time depends on how deep the diver has been, not on how long he has stayed down. After a dive to 500 feet, it is about thirty-six hours.

The diver's traditional routine is a cycle of diving, decompression, and a spell of normal life before diving again. At a depth of 200 feet, requiring a decompression time of eight hours, this was reasonable; but it became uneconomic for the oil companies as they began to drill in deeper waters. The old system, now known as 'bounce diving', was replaced by a new one – 'saturation diving'. The diver comes up and stays in the chamber until he is rested and ready to go down again. As he doesn't emerge into the outside world, it doesn't matter whether he is completely

decompressed or not. The chamber has six bunks for the team of divers, and the one I saw at the Comex school was ten feet long, though a diver told me later that it's bigger than most chambers on the rigs. Food is sent in through a double door. A diver may be in the chamber – or rather, alternately in the chamber and under the sea – for a month.

Comex training school, Aberdeen

It is a strange life. The only comparison is with space travel, but the astronauts have work to do and observations to make – and something to look at – while the divers have nothing to occupy them. They play cards, or they read – 'you'd be amazed how many novels I've read,' said the superintendent. For a man with the right temperament, it's money for jam. But one diver said to me: 'The tension is terrific.' If a man has had a nasty experience on his last dive, he doesn't enjoy sitting in the chamber and thinking about going down again.

When a diver comes out of the chamber, he can't be quite sure of being fully decompressed. If there is still gas in his bloodstream, he is attacked by 'the bends' – a sudden and agonizing pain caused by the rupture of skin or muscle tissues. He goes straight back into the chamber and suffers no permanent harm. One man told me that he endured a terrible few minutes when he got the bends and couldn't draw anyone's attention – this was on a diving-ship, not on a rig. The possible consequences are serious indeed; a spinal bend can produce paralysis of the legs, a cerebral bend leads to a brain haemorrhage which may be fatal. A more insidious risk for the diver is bone necrosis, a slow disease of the bone structure which leads to a condition like arthritis. So far, knowledge of its incidence in deep-water diving and of how to guard against it is inadequate. 'Our problem,' said a diver, 'is that the demands of the industry are advancing faster than medical science.'

The best available figures indicate that twenty-five divers have lost their lives, a large number when one recalls that the number of divers is still less than a thousand. Some deaths have certainly been caused by faulty equipment or by mistakes made on the surface; thus, two divers were sucked into a pipeline section because someone forgot to close a valve. And in September 1975 two divers died from over-heating in the decompression chamber, which is the last thing that ought to happen. However, the general view in the profession is that the risk comes from a diver's own errors. He may stumble on a rock and strain his breathing-pipe, or get it tangled while intent on his work. A diver who had seen two of his friends die said cheerfully: 'You can only kill yourself.' Divers in general are convinced that an experienced man is always safe, and those who die are new divers who 'don't look after themselves'. Of course, the experienced men are most emphatic about this, but almost certainly it contains a good deal of truth, and it underlines the need for proper training. The new Health and Safety Act is making a big difference to the diver's prospects of survival. Equipment has been improved and is tested much more regularly than in earlier years, and divers now have a right to refuse to go down, which is quite a novelty.

Hamilton rig
Below: Control room for the divers' unit

Below: Up into the
diving bell from the
decompression chamber

Bottom: Divers'
decompression chamber

The diver on Pentagone 82 was very reluctant
to talk to me. 'There's a lot of nonsense been
spread about diving being dangerous,' he said.
'You accept the risks if you like the job. It's only
like being a miner or driving a long-distance lorry.'
(Actually, according to the study by the Scottish
doctors, the death rate of divers is thirty-three
times the rate for miners.) I asked why he liked the
job. 'Well, you're independent, you use your own
judgement, everything's up to you. I wouldn't
go back to some ordinary job.'

A more forthcoming character – in fact, he was
delighted to talk – was Rab Butler, a diver whom I
met in an Aberdeen bar. ('Rab Butler, that's right,
like the Chancellor of the Exchequer.') 'The saturation diving's OK when you get used to it. It's a
lot safer than bounce diving – you needn't hurry
to finish the job, you just come up and go back. Oh,
I like the life. Some people like mountains, I like it
down under the sea. You can have some good
jokes. Just on my last trip, there was a ling –
that's a fish – he kept nosing round wondering
what I was doing, then he got into my bell and I
had to pull him out, I got quite friendly with him in
the end. Diving's been my life. I started out in
the Navy. The whole trouble is, they're running
out of Navy divers. You get men going deep
down who've only been scuba-diving, they think
it's just fun, they don't concentrate. It takes
time to make a proper diver. I've had the bends
several times. It's nasty while it lasts but it doesn't
worry me, the chamber's always there. Being
able to refuse to go down if you don't feel hundred
per cent, that's a big advance. The only thing that
does worry me is this necrosis. I'm reading all
I can about it. It's the only thing that might make
me give up diving.'

I had a less reassuring conversation with a
diver, whom I shan't name, in the bar of the

Caledonian Hotel in Peterhead. 'I was a Navy diver, then I came out and I got a decent job right away. A rep in the food trade, that's what I was. But the Navy chaps who dive in the North Sea are always on the lookout for divers. It's a regular network, they don't leave you alone. They wave the magic wand – well, of course, the money's like nothing you've ever seen before. So I let myself get caught. I've been at it two and a half years, but I'm going to give it up, I really am. My wife never sees me. When I'm not actually at sea I'm always on call. I was down in Yarmouth, I couldn't get home for nine months. I'm on call right now.'

'What kind of man becomes a diver, would you say?'

'A bloody idiot.'

'Are you a bloody idiot?'

'Too right I am.'

He's drinking at a tremendous rate, even by the standards of the lounge bar at the Caledonian, the local centre for the better-paid ranks of the oil business. He's working from a pipelaying barge, moored not far from the coast. I think apprehensively of his being called back and diving tomorrow with a hangover. If he isn't an alcoholic now, he will be if he goes on like this; probably that's why he wants to give up diving.

'What do you do with all the money you're earning?'

'What money? I haven't got any money, I never see it. I don't know where it goes.' He has just told me that he makes £150 a day when he's diving. But he hasn't bought a house, he lives in a Council flat, he doesn't own a car, his suit is shabby.

'It doesn't matter what the money is, it's not worth it. That's where I made my big mistake. You're in that chamber, six of you, like in a sausage roll, you just feel you can't bear another minute. But you can't get out, no way. Just down the North Sea again.'

Three pints and three double whiskies later, the barmaid is looking anxious. I ask: 'Where are you staying tonight?'

'How do I know? I might go to the Imperial, the Imperial in Aberdeen, if somebody gives me a lift. I might have to go back to the fucking barge. I can't go home, that's all I know.'

So long as divers are in short supply, they will be lured by 'the magic wand' and they will be well paid. The earnings are fixed by individual negotiation. A man who is prepared to do only bounce diving will get £40 a day. Saturation divers get a minimum of £60, and beyond that the contract depends on the diver's experience and his value to the company. Rab Butler, whose information was reliable – he wasn't a boastful man and he was sober – was making £150. The rate is paid for every day when the diver is aboard a rig, probably about nine months in the year, and unlike a rig-worker he also gets a substantial retainer while ashore. Most of the divers, I was told at the Comex headquarters, establish residence in the Channel Islands or the Isle of Man. Rab had put in a year's diving off the Bahamas and was a legal resident. He was dressed in a denim jacket and jeans, he was drinking half-pints of lager, he lives in a flat in Aberdeen; his income can't be less than £40,000 a year, virtually free of tax. I have certainly never bought a lager for a wealthier man.

I wouldn't be a diver, all the same.

**BP Forties Field: four steel production
platforms in various stages of completion**
Above left: Forties Delta, jacket stage only.
Below left and above right: Forties Charlie and
Bravo. Alongside are derrick barges for handling
construction materials. Below right: Forties Alpha,
which came on stream on 15 September 1975.
Overleaf: Derrick barge and platform

Hamilton Transworld 58 semi-submersible rig

Hamilton Bros. won the oil race by bringing the first oil ashore by tanker

Hamilton rig

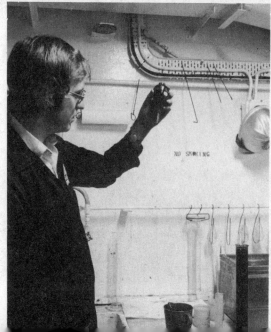

Right: Testing the oil

THE CONCRETE PLATFORM

North Sea Horizons

Top: Pipelaying barge.
Conditions on pipe-
laying barges are
possibly even more
difficult and dangerous
than on the rigs. No
visitors allowed: 'It's far
too dangerous.'

Centre: Materials barge
for transporting pipes,
laid up because of bad
weather

Below: 'Burning off' to
test oil pressure on an
exploration rig

After the rigs, the platforms. They are, so to speak, the siege-guns of the oil war, if the rigs are the charging cavalry. A platform can be made either of steel or of concrete. In the former case it contains as much steel as a battleship; in the latter case as much concrete as a large block of flats, and also a good deal of steel for the strengthening partitions. Firms building the platforms are, distinctly, learning as they go along. Until the North Sea oil boom, platforms were designed to stand in shallower and calmer waters and were very much smaller.

By mid-1975 four platforms had been installed, three for BP and one for the Shell-Exxon consortium. The question of how many there will ultimately be is wide open. In the days when the oil rush was being launched in an atmosphere of breezy optimism, there was talk of eighty platforms; now, one hears estimates of maybe thirty-five. At the construction sites we visited – each in the early stages of building a platform due for completion in 1977 – the workers were acutely aware of the uncertainties. 'We're OK for a couple of years, but what's going to happen then? The company hasn't got another order' – as, in truth, it hadn't. Depressingly, no new orders were placed in the whole of 1975.

To begin with, we've already seen that the scale and pace of the whole North Sea venture are clouded by doubts. Then, the success of Hamilton Brothers in producing from a rig and delivering the oil by tanker, thus dispensing with platforms and pipelines, may mean that other companies will adopt this method, although the 'majors' firmly deny that it would make sense in a large field. Then again, a keen debate rages over the merit of steel and concrete construction, and if purchasers settle decisively for one of these, construction firms equipped for the other could be left high and dry. Finally, as with the rigs, countries other than Britain are bidding for business. With the oil 100 or 150 miles off Scottish shores, it may seem obvious that these bulky structures should be built in Britain – indeed, in Scotland – but geography is not the only consideration. American companies will buy wherever they can get the job done; and the French company, Total (now moving on to the North Sea scene in a big way) is to a large extent state-owned and naturally inclines to have its platforms built at Cherbourg. In mid-1975, out of sixteen platforms on order for work in the British sector of the North Sea, eight were to be built in Britain (six of them in Scotland) and the other eight abroad – four in Norway, three in France, one in the Netherlands. The numbers will be different in 1976, but the proportions will probably be about the same.

The British Government has to give its agreement to the creation of a construction site, and in most cases provides public money for the clearing of the land, for road improvements and for basic services. Often, especially in the Scottish Highlands, the economic benefits must be balanced against the desecration of beautiful scenery and ecological damage. The dilemmas evoke sympathy. If the Government designates too many sites, in relation to the orders ultimately secured, it will be accused of miscalculation and extravagance; if it designates too few, it will be charged with missing chances and causing the work to go to foreign competitors. So far, it has designated eight sites in Scotland and most people I talked to thought that this was too many. At Portavadie, on the lonely shores of Loch Fyne, a firm called Sea Platform Constructors has spent £9 million of the taxpayer's money on levelling a mountainside and hasn't (as I write) secured an order. Portavadie, people were ready to say, is a white elephant, a groundnuts scheme. But of course, it may turn up trumps in the end.

Naturally, it is the construction companies who search for sites in the first place and apply for Government consent and backing; and they too have their dilemmas. There is the problem of the tow-out, which influences oil firms placing orders. From the Highland Fabricators site at Nigg, on the Moray Firth, it's only two hundred miles; from the McAlpine site at Ardyne Point, in the Clyde estuary, it's more like a thousand, through channels that call for careful navigation and round the north coast where the Armada was annihilated. As the towing season is short and a platform travels at less than two miles an hour, this is an important consideration. Then there is the problem of road and rail communications. All roads in Scotland, beyond the central belt where the motorways end, are utterly inadequate even for the tourist traffic, let alone the demands of heavy industry. The A9 from Perth to Inverness is the major horror, and even the improvements now in hand will make it dual-carriageway only for a quarter of its winding 115-mile length. Finally, and one imagines most significantly in some entrepreneurial minds, there is the problem of labour. At Ardyne Point, which is near Dunoon and a familiar ferry-ride from Glasgow, and at construction sites on Tyneside and Teesside in the traditional shipbuilding areas of northeast England, there's an ample supply – especially in these days of unemployment – of workers who already have homes near the job, including trained

welders, boilermakers and the like. These strongholds of industry, however, are also strongholds
of trade unionism. Some companies have clearly
reckoned, though not quite correctly, that they
would find a more tractable spirit among the
simple peasantry of the Highlands, or among
transient workers far from their roots.

The boldest decision, undoubtedly, was to set
up a construction site on the shore of Loch
Kishorn, an inlet of Loch Carron. Loch Carron
is itself a wide fjord set among the mountains
of Wester Ross, the wildest and emptiest countryside in Europe with the exception of Lapland.
The territory behind Loch Kishorn is still described on the map as Applecross Forest, but the
forest was long ago cut down by landlords to
make grouse moors. Here, the Highland clearances
were carried out with utter ruthlessness, an
economy of peasant farming was destroyed, and the
populations of entire villages were driven to find
new homes in Canada. In 1840 the sprawling
county of Ross and Cromarty had a population of
85,000, almost all crofters. Today it is 65,000 – it
has been lower – and is mostly concentrated in the
towns of the Cromarty coast, leaving Wester Ross
a virtual wilderness. Nothing like the platform-
construction site has ever happened here before,
or was ever dreamed of.

The original idea was to locate the site at
Drumbuie, a village on the southern shore of
Loch Carron, more or less facing Loch Kishorn.
The National Trust protested vigorously, and
after a public inquiry and the customary lengthy
controversy, the project was vetoed. This resulted
in two platforms being built in Norway, at a cost
of £110 million to Britain's balance of payments.
Then, apparently considering that the conservation lobby ought to win one round and the
construction industry the next, the Government

agreed to Loch Kishorn. Many people, including lovers of Highland scenery, think that this site is more 'destructive of amenity' than Drumbuie would have been; certainly it's more open to view. The whole affair seems to have been a real old planning muddle. Looking across Loch Kishorn at the construction site, you see what would undoubtedly be an eyesore in the trim, civilized setting of southern England. Here, the huge scale of the landscape reduces it to minor proportions. On a misty day – and there are plenty of misty days – you could easily miss seeing it. Under a clear sky, the mountain called Coir Each looks down impassively. It is broad and rounded like the head of a Highland bull, and the horizontal outcrops of grey rock seem to be lines of rumination; if one may personify a mountain (I became very fond of Coir Each) it makes an impression of immense age, dignity and wisdom. The man-made cliffside of the cavity where the platform is being built reaches a height of 150 feet – but Coir Each rises to 2,500. If I lived here, I thought, I'd object to the construction site chiefly because of the noise. Concrete-mixers, cranes, bulldozers, heavy lorries and pumps throb and groan all day and all night, and the sound travels easily across the water to the villages on the southern shore of Loch Carron. But visually, the offence is diminished to an incident.

Loch Kishorn builds concrete platforms. The firm, Howard-Doris, is one of those international mergers common in the oil business. Howard (the Sir John Howard Group) is a heavy construction company specializing hitherto in building docks, and is responsible for seeing the project through; Doris is a French firm and its contribution is the design. The work in hand is a platform for the Ninian oilfield, up north on a latitude with the

Shetlands. The tow will be a long one, 875 miles, and it will be essential to meet the target date of May 1977.

To reach Loch Kishorn from any direction, you drive for many miles on those single-track roads which are a Highlands speciality, and have to stop

View across Loch Kishorn to construction site

in a passing-bay when anybody is coming in the opposite direction. To supply the construction site by road was therefore an impossibility. Luckily, the railway line from Inverness to Kyle of Lochalsh passes through Strome Ferry, on the south shore of Loch Carron. Supplies are unloaded

here and taken on to the construction site by towed barge, a trip of about two hours depending on the tide. Items which are too bulky for the railway, such as steel sections, come by ship from the Clyde. In the era of the juggernaut lorry, it's reassuring to see trains and ships doing the job that they would have done a century ago. But if British Rail really means to close all its lines north of Glasgow, that will put the construction site out of business.

The origins of Strome Ferry are obvious, since the loch is here at its narrowest point, but the ferry was closed several years ago for want of traffic. The village, missed by the main road and huddled at the foot of a pine-covered mountain, is tiny: a dozen houses, two churches, the sturdy old station, and the dignified Strome Ferry Hotel, which until recently must have been (as an Israeli once said to me of Jericho) the ideal place to re-read *War and Peace*. At the end of 1974, Howard-Doris moved in.

The hotel is now full the year round, a home for Howard-Doris staff. The exiguous area of flat

Strome Ferry railhead

Maiden voyage of cement transporter from Strome Ferry to Kishorn site

land has been increased by reclamation from the loch; jetties and breakwaters have been built; Howard-Doris shunting engines fuss busily along new tracks and sidings. As a vital supply point, Strome Ferry handles anything needed at the construction site from nuts and bolts to food. But its main function is to handle the cement for which the concrete platform has an inexhaustible thirst. Arriving in British Rail tip-up trucks, the cement is fed into four (there will be six) tall silos, and then piped into horizontal containers – silos lying on their sides – which are linked to make an unwieldly but practical barge. Under huge arc-lights, work goes on far into the night. A man who takes a job here can expect to work ten hours a day, seven days a week. It may be fifteen hours, the foreman says – if a train comes along, it's got to be unloaded.

We push on to the construction site, taking the winding road by the head of Loch Carron and then the head of Loch Kishorn – a distance of 24 miles, compared to six as the barge chugs. After we cross the little Kishorn river by a picturesque stone bridge, the public road to Shieldaig vanishes into the mountains (it's the highest road in Britain). We leave it here, and for the last two miles along the shore we use the new road built by Howard-Doris. When we park the car, we're in the midst of a major industrial establishment. It takes half an hour to do a quick preliminary walk round.

The centrepiece is the great circular pit where the platform is being built, known to everyone as The Hole. On the landward side it is framed by a considerable cliff, hung with wire mesh to stop rocks from falling. On the sea-front there's an earthen wall – the bund, they call it – which took weeks to make. A concrete platform has to be built in two stages, occupying about ten months each. Stage One happens in the Hole; the platform gets its floor and rises to a height of 17 metres. Then it's floated out to the deep water of the loch, and during Stage Two it progresses to its ultimate height of 170 metres. (For 'height' read 'depth', once it is sunk into the North Sea; only 31 metres will be above sea-level.) Ideally, the Hole should be enclosed by a lock-gate, like the gate of a dock, to be opened when the time for floating out comes. But at Loch Kishorn the work had to be started

Loch Kishorn construction site

without this refinement, so the laboriously built bund will have to be destroyed after serving its purpose.

Above the Hole, on an artificial plateau, there are concrete-mixers, a generator building, engineering workshops, and stores. The site has no main services and is completely self-sufficient for electricity – the generator supplies enough for a small town, because much of the work will be done after dark – as well as water and sewage. On one side you see the office buildings for managers and draughtsmen, on the other the living quarters for (at the time of our visit) 300 men.

It's the morning of August 8, 1975. Incredibly, on New Year's Day there was absolutely nothing here – nothing but the meditative presence of Coir Each and a hillside descending to the rocky coast. A manager tells me that in the early days he had a two-mile walk (in the dark, of course) every morning and evening. Work on the platform started in July. Getting the Hole dug in six months was a remarkable feat, for it normally takes a year to dig the foundations of a large office building. But the preparation of the site has overlapped with the starting of the platform; roadways and workshops are still under construction, and Howard-Doris workers mingle with the employees of various contracting firms, living in caravans strung out along the approach road. To comply with Scots law, the bar on the site is closed to the contractors' men at ten o'clock, whereas Howard-Doris men are classed as residents and can drink until midnight.

The atmosphere doesn't seem to be one of unremitting toil. As we wander round, workers stop to explain what they're doing, or to chat and ask us questions, without being rebuked by foremen; and there are inevitable delays as they wait for materials. Nevertheless, everyone is conscious of working under pressure. It is Loch Kishorn's first platform, snags are bound to arise, and completion by the target date is by no means a certainty. There are rival sites, after all. If the platform isn't ready on time, there may not be another order; this is the real sanction.

Normally, everyone works a 75-hour week – twelve hours a day from Monday to Friday, seven and a half on Saturday and Sunday. Officially, there is no compulsory overtime. Workers as well as managers assured me that a man can knock off after eight hours' work if he chooses; it's arranged informally in each little team. The management relies on the desire for overtime and bonus money, plus the obvious fact that a man who stops work has nothing to do except lie on his bed or wander about the wild countryside. But what would happen if a man persistently stuck to the legal forty-hour week? An executive said drily: 'His lack of enthusiasm would be noted.'

Very few of the workers are local men and able to live at home, though by chance I ran across one from Applecross, twelve miles away. About half of them come from the Highlands – quite a contingent from Ullapool, a town long plagued by unemployment and lack of opportunity. The rest are from 'southern Scotland' (a term which, from this viewpoint, includes the Clyde and the central belt) or from anywhere in England, Wales and Ireland. Workers whose homes are within reasonable distance take weekends, or just Sundays, off. It's more usual to take a long weekend (Thursday night to Tuesday morning) once a month. There's a type of man who has settled, years ago, for living in work camps, working heavy overtime, and seeing his family only intermittently. He'll work on building a motorway, a bridge, a power station; completion of the project will be followed by a 'break', something between a rest and unemployment, until the next one turns up. Loch Kishorn is a project like any other. But it's a good job, most of them say, and they'll be glad if that second order comes along.

To begin with, there was no trade union. However, as the labour force settled into a community, men with union experience got the site organized, meeting little or no resistance from management. Most of the workers now belong to UCATT, the construction union; indeed, some

Kishorn: Concrete pouring and trowelling

are under the impression that the site is a closed shop, though this isn't strictly true. Industrial relations seem to be cosy, with a desire on both sides to avoid conflict and make the project a success. Frank Routledge, the senior shop steward, is evidently on good terms with Don Findlay, the site manager. 'Mr Findlay is a real gentleman,' he tells me earnestly.

The basic rate is 95 pence an hour. Negotiations have added a site allowance for the unpleasant outdoor conditions and a bonus system. A man who works the customary long hours will gross £150 a week. Clearly, £150 for 75 hours is better than the pay on the rigs, at £120 for 84 hours – and these men are earning the year round, with a right to their basic pay during three weeks' annual holiday. Most of them, I gather from

Kishorn: Site clearance and preparation

random conversations, are well satisfied. A few tell me that it's not enough, conditions are better at other sites, they're forced to keep working in driving rain when they ought to be able to knock off and get paid for 'wet time'. When I quote this to Routledge he says: 'I know that little lot. Trouble-makers.' To his mind, evidently, they are

Top: Putting the steel
skirts into position,
Kishorn. Below:
Teabreak, Kishorn.
Right: Teabreak. The
wire netting covering the
cliff behind is to stop
rockfalls

disrupting the harmony of Loch Kishorn.

One man with wide experience of construction work takes a balanced view. 'You can always push the wages up on a job like this if the management can't afford interruptions and if you've got real cunning shop stewards. I was on the Shell refinery at Birkenhead. You could pull in three hundred nicker without even working hard. It was done by theoretical hours, going by the amount of concrete that got spread. I've chalked up two hundred hours a week – theoretical, mind. The shop stewards here aren't up to all the tricks. Still, they're good lads, they're learning. I've got a wife and two kids, I'm sending home a hundred a week after tax. I'm not grumbling.'

Planning permission for the site was based on the number of men to be employed, which governed the acreage used. Howard-Doris' application stated a work-force of 400. Within six months this had (with the inclusion of contractors' men) been exceeded. Critics say that the company was pulling a fast one; the Howard-Doris version is that the platform they were asked to build, and therefore the dimensions of the Hole, were bigger than they'd expected. Anyway, the permitted work-force has now been raised to 850. Faced with the demands of the oil boom, a mere planning officer in Wester Ross had no option.

The project begins with the construction of the base of the platform. First the steel skirts, to ensure stability at sea, are put in. Then the timber support, a job for joiners and carpenters; it will be left behind, of course, when the platform is moved. Then the base itself – 17,000 cubic metres of concrete, with steel strengthening. It's marked out in sections, and at this early stage the Hole looks curiously like an archaeological dig, especially when you gaze down from the top of the cliff. Surveyors are sighting from triangulators, some men are fixing tapes to indicate the sections, others are making walk-ways with planks, and others crouch on the ground, smoothing the cement with trowels. When the site is in final shape the cement will be piped from the silos, but I saw it being brought in mixer-lorries, lurching down a rocky track which bulldozers were still trying to smooth.

Once the base is completed, work will start on the uprights, enclosed in wooden forms which will move up on hydraulic jacks. But most of this belongs to Stage Two and will be done out in the loch.

Throughout Stage One, water will be a continuing problem. Even when I was there, after weeks of the sunniest and driest summer that Scotland can remember, the Hole was muddy in places. Water from the mountainside seeps through the rock-bed; more water from the loch seeps in through the bund. Fifteen diesel pumps are working day and night, contributing the loudest notes in the cacophany of sound. Other portable pumps will be needed when wet weather sets in.

Clocking off, after twelve hours' work

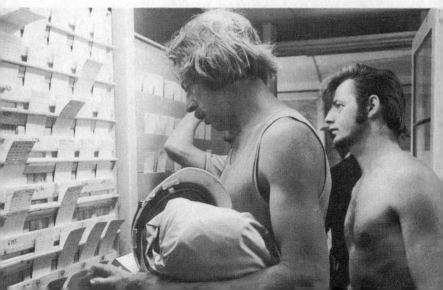

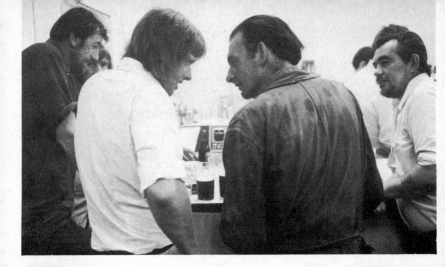

Kishorn: the bar and the midges

But from the workers' point of view the main handicap is the rough climate. It's seldom very cold in the West Highlands, but the winds are strong and it can rain for weeks. A man who had arrived in early spring said to me in an awed tone: 'Have you ever seen horizontal rain? You will here.' It doesn't, to put the matter mildly, make the

Kishorn: new bar
nearly completed

job of spreading cement any easier.

Summer comes as a distinctly mixed blessing. Down in the Hole, which faces south, there's no shade except just under the cliff and seldom the vestige of a breeze. The day before I arrived, when holiday-makers were rejoicing at temperatures in the eighties, a thermometer in the Hole gave a shade reading of ninety-eight. Also, the north-west of Scotland is notoriously infested by clouds of midges. Breeding in the stagnant seeping water and attracted by sweat, they are out in full strength both in the morning and the evening, so a man working a twelve-hour day will have them round his head for a good four hours. Your face is itching, your eyes are watering from dust, your hands are sticky with cement, you carry your midge-cloud wherever you go . . . you've earned your £150.

Managers say that it's too early to give any figures of labour turnover. Talking to workers individually and in groups, I got the impression that they were undecided about sticking it out. A man would tell me that he was in a good job and happy with his earnings, and express concern about the prospects beyond 1977; a minute later, he would say: 'Mind you, I'm not sure how long I'm staying.'

An electrcian, wiring up the engineering workshops: 'They're all right, these steel-frame buildings. You get the walls and roof on in four weeks, then they keep you out of the rain. I'm doing the usual hours, I can pull in a hundred and seventy pounds. It's a fierce place, though. The road was blocked by snow on the second of June, you know that? I might stop for a year. Depends on what else is going.'

A man putting up the steel framework, employed by Allen Fabricators of Tewkesbury, says in his soft west-country accent: 'I'm temporary here, of course. I'll be glad to see civilization again. It's bloody terrible here, it really is. Miles from the nearest pub, and that's not a proper pub, sort of a hotel. And these blasted midges! They're going too fast, that's my opinion. Just today a lorry backed on to a stack of my frames, ruined the lot of them. It's not a normal life here, not a bit normal.'

A young man putting up fencing round the perimeter: 'Oh, I'm enjoying it. But then, I'm just here for the summer. I'm an architecture student. I don't get the bonus, but I'm still making £115 a week. There's seven of us here, students. Mostly they're on catering, so they're not making so much, but they all like it. A good atmosphere, very friendly.'

A cementer: 'It's a good site, better than most. You've got to work, but you're trusted, you can set your own pace. I'm saving, that's what I like – I've never spent less in my life. I reckon I'll stay till Christmas. After that, I'll see.'

The work-camp stands on high ground inland from the Hole. As prefab buildings go, these are not unattractive; a Council housing estate would clash more stridently with the landscape. Each man has a reasonably pleasant room, and the central feature of this isolated community is the big amenity block. The company, naturally, has an interest in making a reality of the word 'amenity' and thus reducing the labour turnover. 'We're trying to provide everything but crumpet,' the manager said. What between the sparseness of the population and the puritanical traditions of this part of Scotland, crumpet is indeed scanty. In other respects, Howard-Doris does its workers proud.

There's a film every night, and live entertainment – usually a folk-singer or a comedian – once a week, all free. At present these are in the canteen, but it's planned to build a cinema with a sloping floor and comfortable seats, and also a gym with judo and aikido instructors. There are thoughts, too, of company boats to be made available for fishing trips. The amenity block has a billiard-room, a barber-shop, a launderette, two shops, a bank and a post office. If you can't have 'civilization', this is the next best thing.

The canteen is run cafeteria-style, but deserves the name of restaurant. For the evening meal when I was there, the choice was between spaghetti bolognese, chicken fricassee, and gammon and pineapple. The cost of full board and lodging is £11.90 a week; clearly, it is subsidized with a view to attracting and keeping workers. A man who doesn't drink or smoke can save, or send home to his family, nine tenths of his wages.

The bar, as I saw it, was small and crowded, and very hot on an August night; but a much bigger bar was being fitted up. You could drink a lot at Loch Kishorn – having a bar so close to your

room, and open till midnight, is an obvious temptation – and undoubtedly some of the men do. But most of them, or so I was assured, find that hangovers and twelve-hour work shifts don't go together. One man, who admitted to going through a bottle of whisky a day when he's at home and not working, told me: 'By the time I've knocked off, and had a shower and a meal, and read my paper, I don't feel like starting on the drink.

Saturday night in Loch Carron hotel bars, several miles from Kishorn site. Very few girls

It's doing me a lot of good, this place is.'

Finally, the amenity block has a trim little clinic, staffed by four trained nurses and with local doctors coming in every day. The site has its own ambulances, as well as its own fire-engines; the nearest hospital is at Inverness, a long way off, but it runs a helicopter service (not just for Loch Kishorn – this is a regular feature of the National Health Service in the Highlands). Considering the pace of work, the Howard-Doris safety record

is good. In the early days, a lorry working on building the bund slid into the sea and the driver was drowned. Nobody could call to mind any disasters, or serious injuries, since then.

Life at Loch Kishorn is decidedly congenial for the staff – thirty-six managers and office-workers. They live in hotels, and avail themselves of the canteen and bar in the amenity block; shortly, they are to get a restaurant and bar of their own.

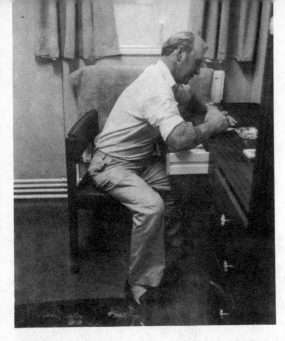

Letter-writing

The company is building a couple of dozen 'executive-type' houses near the little town of Lochcarron, seven miles from the construction site. They look solid and spacious and they'll have a marvellous view. One manager said that the proposed rent was a bit steep, at £12 a week. But he came from Ullapool, and cheered up when I told him what he'd be paying in London, and for that matter in Aberdeen.

Like everything else connected with North Sea oil, Loch Kishorn is a gamble. The outlay – partly at the expense of Howard-Doris, partly in Government aid – has been enormous. Nobody is going to put the landscape back as it was before. The Hole could become a swimming-pool, and the work-camp a holiday-camp, but in this remote spot and in the generally chancy climate such a venture wouldn't be hopeful. There's no telling how many concrete platforms will be built here, or built at all. Loch Kishorn may have a useful life of ten years – in the worst case, only two years. One can only hope for the best.

THE STEEL PLATFORM

Driving from Wester Ross to Easter Ross – from the Atlantic coast to the coast of the North Sea – we traverse miles of lonely and mountainous moorland. At last we reach a gentler landscape, where the countryside has long been tamed to man's use. There is good farming land in the valleys of the beautiful rivers, and also on Black Isle, a broad protrusion between Cromarty Firth and Moray Firth. The little towns – Beauly, Dingwall, Invergordon, Tain – have a peaceful and contented air. There seems no reason why Easter Ross should not be prosperous; however, it never has been. No ports, either for trade or fishing, developed along the Firths, and industry was deterred by poor communications through the Inverness bottleneck. Invergordon, the largest town, depended on its naval base and that was closed down in 1957; perhaps it had never been trusted since the 1931 mutiny. For a bitter decade, the employment outlook was hopeless.

By 1970, the decline had been halted. Invergordon acquired a large aluminium plant, an equally substantial engineering works and a paper mill. Then the news broke that a sheltered beach on Nigg Bay, close to the narrows where Cromarty Firth joins the open sea, had been chosen as a site for building oil platforms made of steel. Two platforms have now been completed at Nigg and work has begun on a third. But men who had been driven south by unemployment have returned to their home country, and some of the new jobs have gone to incomers, to use the handy Scots word. So there is still some unemploy-

Coastline scenery near Nigg

ment in Easter Ross, though less than the national average.

The Nigg peninsula, jutting ten miles across the mouth of the Firth, is mostly flat. Often it's covered by a dense white mist, known as the haar (a Norwegian word) and as you probe your way along the quiet roads you seem to have moved out of the modern world, an impression enhanced

by the many crumbling structures – aircraft hangars and gun emplacements – which are relics of the last war. Just at the tip of the peninsula, the Hill of Nigg rises to a sudden 600 feet and shuts out the offshore winds. Down on the bay, the weather is calm and can be hot when the sun breaks through the haar.

Few people ever came to Nigg Bay, which is a

nature reserve much prized by bird-watchers. The beach was loved by the discerning, and there were laments when the construction site was planted right on top of it. There is an imposing mansion, once the home of Eric Linklater, now used for entertaining visitors of stature in the oil world. There is the Nigg Ferry Hotel, the only place within lunch-hour reach of the site for a drink and a snack. (The ferry, coming from Black Isle, went out of use years ago, but has been revived to bring workers from that direction.)

Nigg Bay construction site

And there's a scattering of stone-built houses, some in ruins, others still inhabited by people who chose them for a peaceful retirement and have stayed despite the startling change in the environment.

The Nigg site belongs to Highland Fabricators, a partnership between Brown and Root – a major American construction firm with headquarters at Houston, Texas, and much involved in the oil scene, for instance by laying pipelines – and Wimpeys. The Americans, with their considerable experience, took a major hand at the outset in directing operations, and at one time there were 160 of them at Nigg as executives, supervisors or instructors; now there are about forty. Two platforms have been built for BP's Forties field. Highland One, taking two years' work, was completed in 1973. Highland Two was finished in eighteen months and towed out in June 1975, a

Top right: Houston time – and GMT. Top left: US supervisor at Nigg. Above: US visiting engineer

Nigg : Early stages of construction of steel platform at Nigg
Top: Platform construction protected from the elements
Centre: Japanese steel being unloaded from a German freighter
Below: Woman welder

triumphant six weeks ahead of schedule. A month later, work began on a platform destined, like the one at Loch Kishorn, for the Ninian field. It is to be delivered in May 1977.

This method of construction has no Stage One and Stage Two, for the whole platform is assembled in one place. Having less displacement than a concrete platform, a steel one can be completed before it is floated out. The counterpart to Loch Kishorn's Hole is therefore an enormous dock, enclosed by the largest concrete gate in the world. The dock is supposed to be dry in readiness for work on a new platform, but after the floating-out of Highland Two there was some trouble in getting it empty. When we saw it, it looked like an outsize and regrettably dirty swimming-pool.

Making a steel platform, as opposed to concrete, is an engineering rather than a constructional project. The workers belong to the AUEW, the Boilermakers' Union and the Sheet Metal Workers' Union, not to UCATT. The body of the platform, a huge steel cylinder, is known as the jacket, and the other main components are the mighty legs, reminiscent of those of the Eiffel Tower. Intriguingly, the platform is built on its side and towed to its destination like that. Then pontoons are inflated to tip it upright, and it settles down with an impressive splash.

Nigg has a rolling-mill and makes its own steel, except for flat steel plate. This comes from Japan – 'thanks to the failure of the British Steel Corporation', as our guide said acidly. (His patriotic feelings were further injured by the fact that the steel plate which had just arrived had been trans-shipped in Antwerp instead of London and was being delivered by a German freighter.) Once the steel parts are made, there's a lengthy process of welding and riveting them as the plat-

Portmahomack, near Nigg, almost deserted before the oil boom: the now flourishing hotel charges £140 per week, and is constantly booked by visiting executives from all over the world, like these Japanese steel men

form takes shape; some of this is done in work-shops, most of it in the dock. In the later stages, building a platform is much like building a ship.

Steel construction also differs from concrete in that it requires a much bigger labour force, and a labour force which expands steadily in the course

128

of the project. Just before the completion of Highland Two, Nigg provided 3,500 jobs. About 200 of the workers (aside from office and catering staff) were women. However, jobs for women are scarce in the region, with Nigg and the aluminium smelter as the main employers, and this is one reason for the persistent unemployment, not to mention the below-average family incomes. We met a female welder who had established herself successfully in the workshops, but was meeting resistance from both management and unions to her request to work out of doors on the main structure of the platform. 'Men are more impervious to the elements,' a shop steward told me gravely.

A work-force of this size obviously confronts the district with a considerable housing problem. Engineers and similar industrial workers don't have the migratory habits of construction men; they expect to get homes, not to live from project to project in work-camps. But in the early days they had to put up with what they could get. In seaside villages like Balintore and Portmahomack, which had catered for many years to a modest holiday trade, Nigg brought a bonanza. Rooms, caravans and chalets normally let for six weeks in summer were filled the year round, and some of them still are. In the towns, too, every spare bed was pressed into service. Men were sleeping six to a room, day-shift and night-shift workers were accommodated on the Box and Cox system, and there were many complaints of overcharging. Caravans multiplied all over the countryside, some of them parked by arrangement with farmers, others on waste land.

In an effort to cope with the crisis, the company bought two old ships and moored them at Nigg Ferry. About 400 men lived aboard; it was handy for the construction site and the bar of the Nigg

Portmahomack: only a few yards away from the heavily used disco bar, the camp site still insists on 'no games on Sunday'

Greek ship once used to
accommodate Nigg
workers

Ferry Hotel, but miles from the nearest shop.
The ships proved to be more trouble than they
were worth to Highland Fabricators; they
brought a crop of newspaper stories about over-
crowding and unhealthy conditions – stories
stoutly denied by company spokesmen. I don't
know what truth there was in these allegations,
for the ships have now been sold off, much to the
relief of all concerned. Recently the company has
built a work-camp, or 'beach-camp' as it's en-
ticingly called, on land reclaimed from the sea
alongside the construction site, for workers
temporarily employed at peak production times.
I saw it empty and I can't say accurately what it
would be like to live in, but it's far from pleasing
to the eye – the prefab units are assembled one
above another like packing-cases – and it has
nothing to compare with Loch Kishorn's amenity
block. Still, it's fair to remember that men are
supposed to live there only for a few months, not
for the entire construction period of a platform.

There are still signs of pressure on housing.
When I took a bed-and-breakfast room for a few

Nigg beach camp for construction workers

nights in Tain, another room in the small house was home to a Nigg worker. I came across a couple paying £16 a week for an old farm cottage which had been let for £3 a few years back. Scores of families are living in caravans, mostly on permanent sites with adequate services, but a few gipsy-fashion in odd corners of the countryside. I'm prepared to believe, however, that people living in such conditions are doing so by their own choice. For the District Council is one of the few in Britain to have dealt successfully with its housing problem.

This has been achieved largely through the energy of Councillor John Robertson, who at the crucial time was chairman (or convenor, as it's called in Scotland) of the Housing Committee. Robertson is one of the local people who have welcomed the construction site from the start, somewhat remarkably considering that he has a home and a farm within noise-pollution distance of it. Under his guidance, the Council decided to get a thousand houses built, and get them built quickly. This was done, in the first place, by grouping them in three large estates – at Invergordon, Alness and Balintore – instead of scattering them. (One advantage of this policy is that company buses get the workers to and from Nigg by using a small number of collection-points.) It was done, above all, by buying five hundred factory-made timber-frame houses. A house like this can be assembled in a day, and the services for a whole street can be connected within a week. As a result, the programme of a thousand houses was started in May 1974 and completed in May 1975. An applicant can now get a Council house in six weeks, or less than that if he doesn't mind which of the estates he goes to.

These timber-frame houses look very attractive, I thought, and are quite free from the shed-like appearance that one associates with prefabs. At Balintore in particular – where the estate is well designed, with crescent-shaped streets and plenty of traffic-free play space for the children – they make a pleasant village-like environment. People seem to be delighted with them; they are superbly insulated, one woman said with awe that she could keep warm with one electric bar (a new experience in a Scottish winter), and therefore the fuel bills are low. They cost the Council about the same as conventional brick-built houses. In fact, the only thing wrong with them is that they have to be bought from Norway. No British firm is prepared to supply them, although Scotland is covered with pine-forests.

The Council has done such a splendid job that it seems unjust to cavil, but some disadvantages have followed from the transformation of what used to be small and neighbourly communities. Alness, especially, is reeling from the shock. Not long ago it was a village of eight hundred souls; now it is a town of eight thousand, thanks to the Council estate and to ready planning permission for a great deal of private building. The

Top: Norwegian
prefabs at Alness
Left: Private house
building at Alness

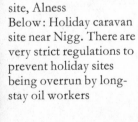

Left: Residential caravan
site, Alness
Below: Holiday caravan
site near Nigg. There are
very strict regulations to
prevent holiday sites
being overrun by long-
stay oil workers

road authorities haven't helped by changing the signs so that the A9 now runs through Alness instead of Invergordon. The schools are lagging behind the houses, as they generally do, and just beginning to catch up by the use of emergency classrooms. There are no community buildings and practically no entertainment. 'There's nothing to do here but get drunk, so we all do,' one man told us frankly but not happily. We didn't have a free evening to test this assertion, but everyone we asked said that it was true.

One way and another, there's a certain amount of tension in and around Nigg. Partly, this arises from the influx of thousands of strangers – inevitable, although it has been company policy to employ local people by preference. It's one thing for a Scot at Loch Kishorn to have a Birmingham man in the next room, when both are construction workers used to living away from home, and another for a native of Alness, perhaps earning low wages in some traditional occupation, to find that his new neighbour is an incomer with a thicker wage-packet and different social habits. For instance, Easter Ross has strict religious traditions, on the defensive but not extinct, and some people regard drinking – all drinking, not just heavy drinking – as sinful. Partly too, the tension stems from uncertainty about the future of the oil boom; is it worth making expensive social adjustments if it'll be all over in ten years? And partly, it spreads from the distrust, which not long ago took the form of conflict, between Highland Fabricators and its workers.

The first year after the site opened saw a head-on collision between the (mainly American) management and the unions, resulting in several strikes. The company version of this history is that the Americans didn't understand British attitudes. However, with true American pragmatism, they made the necessary adjustment and said to the shop stewards: 'OK, boys, tell us what you want and we'll see what can be done.' As a result, industrial relations are now excellent.

The bit about the American lack of understanding rings true enough. One Brown & Root man said to me carefully: 'The bonus wasn't an easy concept for us to accept. When you pay a man his wages you're just buying his presence, then you pay him some more to work – we're not used to that.' A supervisor, in the rich accent of Baytown, Texas, expounded his philosophy with greater force. 'A man ought to know that if he doesn't give satisfaction he'll be out and there's another man waiting to come in. And he ought to know that if he doesn't work there's no other way to feed his family.' These notions take the British worker back to what he's heard from his father, of the pre-war years when the sack was a constant threat and unemployment meant dire poverty; and the return of high unemployment has sharpened the menace. The opposition here is between a management concept of 'the right to hire and fire' and a trade-union concept of victimization.

Bill Lindsay, the shop stewards' convenor, demurs at the company version of events. 'They came to the Highlands with the deliberate intention of running a non-union yard. It's not because

Nigg steel-rolling mill

they're Americans – it's because they're Brown and Root. They're notorious world-wide. Basically those strikes weren't about bonus payments or anything else; they were about union recognition, and it took us a year of hard fighting to get it. And I get a bit irritated with the way the company keeps telling people like you that relations are so wonderful now. I'd say they're just normal. A fair understanding, that's what it comes down to.' There was no doubt of the implication that the fair understanding depended on the strength and vigilance of the unions.

Wages, according to Lindsay, are 'a hell of a lot better than they were'. The basic rates are satisfactory, but some of the negotiable extras could be improved. I found a welder's helper getting £1.10 an hour; an engineer told me that the top rate for craftsmen is £1.60. 'There might be a few allowances on top of that,' he added, and evidently there are, for a man I met later (the same man who told me that everyone gets drunk in Alness) said that he was making £2 an hour in the rolling-mill. The company also paid bonuses on the completion of the platforms, amounting to £300 for an average worker and £1,000 for a foreman. A lot of this money went in tax, so the unions are now asking for it to be spread over weekly pay-packets instead of coming in a lump sum. From the company's angle, however, the completion bonus is a means of keeping a stable work-force. In the early days, turnover has been as high as 120% in a year.

Kevin Barry, director and founder of Highland Fabricators

'You might say it's a good job,' Lindsay conceded without much enthusiasm. 'It's a good part of the country, and now the lads are settled in they appreciate the housing and the schools. But there's no long-term security.'

Security . . . the word kept cropping up. One aspect of it was a concern about overtime. This

The bar at Nigg Ferry Hotel, where Highlands Fabricators management go to drink

concern isn't primarily financial; one man said his rent was reasonable, there was nothing to spend money on where he lived, and he managed perfectly well on his pay for a forty-hour week. But overtime is a measure of the accelerating or decelerating rhythm of the oil boom.

When Highland One was being built, most men were working 70 hours a week (the workforce was still being recruited, and the company wasn't sure of completing its first platform on time). On Highland Two, they worked 48 hours. There are three eight-hour shifts, as usual when steel is being handled, and the workers also came in on Sundays; they voted to choose Saturdays as the day off because Sundays are so dead in this austere part of Scotland. Now they work a straight 40 hours. Except on the pumps and a few other jobs, no overtime is on offer. At the end of July, the whole site closed down for a fortnight's holiday – something that would be unthinkable at Loch Kishorn.

After the completion of Highland Two, a great

many workers were laid off. This is easily explained by company spokesmen. There is a basic work-force of 1,300 (plus 350 office staff) to whom Highland Fabricators has a commitment of continuing employment; others who may be taken on, to swell the payroll to its peak of 3,500, understand that they don't belong to this 'regular army'. The shop stewards accept this system in principle but say that there were more redundancies than they'd expected. The company, it seems, had promised that local men would be kept on, but when it came to the point there was some disagreement about who was a local man – did he have to live within twenty miles, or within fifty, or what? There is a strict order of priorities, agreed to by the unions, for re-employment: local men first, then Highlanders, then other Scots, then men from northern England, then from the Midlands or Wales, and men from southern England last of all. Whether the work-force on the new platform will reach anything like 3,500 again, no one is sure.

Even the casual visitor could see that work on the new platform, in its early stages, was proceeding at a very leisurely pace. There was a perfectly good reason for this: Howard-Doris don't know that they can build a concrete platform in two years without intensive effort, but Highland Fabricators do know from experience that they can build a steel one in the time. There were practical reasons for a slow start too, such as the trouble with emptying the dock. The lack of haste, however, was being linked in some minds with the question: 'after 1977, what?' – was the company taking it easy because the North Sea wouldn't want anything like thirty-five platforms? In the office, some pains were taken to explain to me that, with its rolling-mill and welding-shops, the site is equipped to take on other projects besides building platforms.

Local opinion – at all events, working-class opinion – holds strongly that Nigg isn't enough to guarantee a durable full-employment economy in the region. There was much talk of a proposal to build an oil refinery on the Nigg peninsula, which would mean about 2,000 jobs during the construction period and 400 permanent jobs. A committee had been formed to lobby for the scheme, and telephone poles along the roads were plastered with posters reading 'Support Cromarty Oil Refinery', with the initial letters enlarged to form the word SCOT. It could bring pollution, but men facing possible unemployment were in no mind to worry about that.

OIL CAPITAL

Every time I came to Aberdeen – from the south, from Nigg, from the North Sea, from the Shetlands – I felt the pleasurable excitement of arriving in a real city. If anything about the oil rush gives the observer a sense of the fitting, it is the designation of Aberdeen as 'Britain's oil capital'. As one walks along Union Street, the main thoroughfare, one has the impression of being in the capital of a small, but not a poor or a humble, nation: a capital with style and character, like Dublin or Amsterdam or Oslo. The civic buildings look like Ministries; the university looks like a university (not a factory, like most British universities); the castle looks like a royal residence, though as a matter of fact it was built by the Salvation Army. Union Street, a mile long, is one of the finest streets in Europe. With the confidence and boldness typical of Victorian building, it was raised

high across a ravine through which the railway
line was made to pass. There are squares and
crescents that delight the eye with their perfection
of scale. The whole city is built of grey granite,
which gives a noble air of solidity, and until quite
recently building with anything else was forbidden.
The richer streets are a worthy habitation for the
Aberdonian bourgeoisie, a class more inclined to
dignity and a sense of proportion than to osten-
tation. Nobody in Aberdeen ever seems to have
minded living in the same kind of house as his
neighbours, and this outlook – along with the
granite – made for stylistic unity. The working-
class districts never had the squalid slums that
disfigured Edinburgh and Glasgow. No mean
city, indeed. The pseudo-architects of office
blocks and high-rise flats are now trying hard to
make Aberdeen look just like anywhere else, but
they will have their work cut out.

It's also unlikely that Aberdeen, whose collective temperament is averse to heady enthusiasms,

**Seaton Estate
Aberdeen**

Aberdeen

will ever be overwhelmed by the oil boom.
Indeed, one could pay quite a lengthy visit without
being made aware of North Sea oil at all. With
185,000 people, Aberdeen is big enough to absorb
a new development which it didn't desperately
need and on which it prefers not to depend.
Employment is pretty well balanced between
the harbour with its trawlers, fish-processing, a
couple of shipyards, a big Michelin factory, and a
good many white-collar jobs in administration and
in a university with several research institutes. The
tone of community life is set, on the whole, not by
businessmen but by professional people – lawyers
(who seem to be exceptionally numerous and
influential), clergy, doctors, university staff,
teachers. The Council, with a safe Labour majority,
is in favour of oil but not in favour of the whole
place being run for the benefit of the oil companies.
Labour and trade-union opinion is cogently
expressed by the North Sea Oil Action Committee, whose spokesman is Bob Middleton,

Aberdeen

the narrowly defeated Labour candidate for Aberdeen South (Aberdeen North is a Labour seat). 'We welcome oil,' he said in a speech in 1975, 'since we believe that it can create a second industrial revolution in this country, and if I and my committee have any purpose at all it is to ensure that we as a nation have learned from the mistakes that were made in the first industrial revolution . . . poor working conditions, poor living conditions, and a general reduction in the quality of life.'

In Aberdeen it isn't easy to see who is working 'in oil'. The rig-workers who come ashore don't look distinctive, few have homes in Aberdeen, and they don't necessarily spend their off-duty time there. It's true that Aberdeen is the directing centre of the oil rush, and this has brought thousands of incomers – the mainly English staff of Shell and BP, the Americans, and people from a dozen European nations. But manager and technicians in the oil business are transferred at frequent intervals between Houston and Aberdeen and Abu Dhabi, and some never get out of the hotels. When they do acquire houses, it's generally in new developments added to outlying villages, or near the airport. They don't get much involved in Aberdeen life, either because it's the custom in the oil world to create self-contained communities, or simply because they are not staying long enough. For instance, there is an American school for the oil children. For social purposes, they gather at the Petroleum Club, an American-style country club. Apparently there are five thousand Americans in and around Aberdeen, but from any signs in the streets and shops and pubs one would never believe it. Except for the contacts I needed for this book, I saw only a few Americans all the time I was there, and they were tourists quite unconnected with the oil business.

Signs of the oil rush in Aberdeen are to some extent absorbed by the large permanent population

The oil boom has impelled visiting journalists to look for a scene of lavish spending, heavy drinking and prostitution, and in 1975 *Newsweek* gave Aberdeen the name of 'Sin City'. This was strongly resented, and my own impression is that anyone in search of a northern Beirut or Bangkok is in for a disappointment. Pubs near the harbour are crowded and lively, and some have gone in for a modern style with pop groups or taped music, 'intimate' lighting and drinks like bacardi and campari, but the young men in these pubs mostly seem to be accompanied by their girl-friends, or their wives for all that I know. In the rougher pubs there are girls on the lookout for men; however, they are generally what were called in wartime 'good time girls' rather than professionals. There are no street-walkers, and there are no bars whose function is to be centres of prostitution, as in many ports throughout the world. Certainly there are prostitutes frequenting the hotels associated with the oil business, and someone who knows the city can name the hotels where a roustabout, a tool-pusher or a company executive would find a girl at the price suited to his income and status. 'We get a better class of prostitute nowadays,' Bob Middleton informed me, speaking of course in his capacity as a magistrate. It's said that a number of expensive 'escort girls' have moved from Mayfair to Aberdeen – from Arab oil money to North Sea oil money, so to speak. The fact remains that sin in Aberdeen tends to be discreet, and doesn't offend the eye of the respectable citizen as he makes his way along Union Street. You would have to make inquiries to find a strip club, a sex shop or a porn shop, which can't be said of English provincial cities like Manchester or Birmingham.

About the drinking, too, one needs to be cautious. Walking along Regent Quay after the pubs close (ten o'clock in Scotland), you're sure to see men who are very drunk indeed. But Aberdeen was always a hard-drinking town, and you don't know who is off the rigs and who is off a trawler. Perhaps the waiting taxis, whose task is almost that of an ambulance, are the best evidence that there's money round the harbour. By eleven, even on a mild summer night, everything is quiet. Some Aberdonians say that the oil boom has made a difference – 'our drunks could always get home, but these roughnecks pass out in the street,' an elderly man told me disapprovingly. Others say it's no worse than it always was.

Holding the title of 'oil capital' has undoubtedly brought money to Aberdeen, but through scores of small channels, not from a single source like the construction site at Nigg. I heard it said that there are three ways to make money out of the oil boom – own a big house and go into the bed-

The Petroleum Club, most of whose members are American, is so exclusive that the sign has even been taken down

Top: The new Sheraton Inn, near the airport

Right: The Americans tend to shop at the wholesalers who supply the rigs, which helps keep them apart from Aberdeen life

Right: Signs of American influence near the Petroleum Club

Below: The American school, Peterculter

and-breakfast business, own a pub, or drive a taxi.
It's to the advantage of Aberdeen, of course, that
all the eggs are not in one basket. The lack of a new
order at Nigg could make Easter Ross a zone of
unemployment; no single blow could be devastat-
ing for Aberdeen, and the worst that could
happen would be a slow dwindling of activity
if one company headquarters or one supply fleet
after another ceased operations. The atmosphere
I found was one of satisfaction, though not of
complacency or even of complete confidence.
Things are pretty good, most people would say,
at a time when they might be pretty bad, for the
general reason that Britain is in a difficult economic
situation and for the particular reason that North
Sea fishing is in a decline. Wages are at the national
average, and earnings are probably above it
because of overtime – both were below average
for most of Aberdeen's history. Where Aberdeen
emphatically scores over the rest of the country is
that it has virtual full employment – or it had when
I was there in August 1975. John McConnachie,
district secretary of the AUEW, told me that he
didn't know of a single factory that had cut back
labour, despite the national situation. An illumin-
ating fact reported in the local paper was that no
one could be found for the job of patrol man or
woman at a dangerous crossing between a housing
estate and a school. The police put up posters
appealing for someone to take the job, but without any success by the beginning of term.

With its balanced economy, Aberdeen – unlike
most Scottish towns – has had nothing worse than
3% unemployment since the last war. But the
figure could have been higher if young men hadn't
gone south to look for work, and the worrying
fact was that unemployment didn't go below 3%
in periods of national prosperity. The city failed to
attract new industrial development – 'we had

Aberdeen at night

Changes of plan and the weather make food supply to the rigs difficult: 'The waste breaks your heart. You could feed the whole of Biafra with it. We recently had to throw away a whole container of rotting food *and* had to pay over £50 to have it cleaned' – wholesale supplier to the rigs

become accustomed to being a backwater,' Bob Middleton says. That, beyond a doubt, has changed. North of Aberdeen at Balgownie, and to the south at Kincorth, new industrial estates present an encouraging picture.

Aberdeen has kept employment high mainly as the chief supply base for the rigs. The harbour has been modernized so that it handles shipping round the clock, instead of only at high tide. Nearby, a new supply base has been built for Amoco. The supply boats employ hundreds of seamen, more and more dockers are needed, ship-repair yards are busy. The main shipyard has a contract for five Navy patrol boats, designed to protect the rigs. To this, one must add a good deal of white-collar employment in the offices of the various oil companies, shipping lines, air charter companies and other enterprises connected with North Sea oil.

By comparison, oil-related industrial employment isn't what was hoped for. In 1973, Baker Tools, an American company, opened a new factory at Balgownie making equipment for the oilfields. It employs 140 men, mostly skilled engineers as the products are highly sophisticated and the factory has its own toolroom. I noticed as I walked round that some at least of the machines are British, and I was told that British steel is beginning to arrive two years after it was ordered. But other buildings at Balgownie which look like factories turn out to be storage and maintenance depots. Sites at the Kincorth estate haven't been taken by new factories so much as by firms moving out of antiquated premises in the city centre. So far as manufacturing industry is concerned, the oil boom has helped to keep employment high by a spread of contracts and sub-contracts to existing firms – anything from waterproof jackets to paint – much more than by bringing in new enterprises.

Full employment but . . . and there are three but's in Aberdeen. Most of the jobs – all that loading and unloading – are unskilled. Very few jobs have been created for women, except in office work: construction and dock work are male occupations, and Baker Tools – the one genuine example of oil-related industry – has so far employed only men. Finally, there's the usual question: how long will it last? The construction phase, with the harbour improved and the Amoco base built, is almost over. There will be fewer platforms than rigs, fewer supply-boats. Baker Tools looks like a permanent acquisition, for it is producing equipment for the Middle East as well as the North Sea. But Aberdeen would like to have a dozen Baker developments, and no more have arrived.

Paradoxically, while far-sighted Aberdonians worry about a future slackening of employment, some firms are crying out for labour. At the Hall Russell shipyard, which is building the patrol boats, the managing director told me that he'd been obliged to turn down another good contract

Baker Oil Tools

Baker Oil Tools

because he can't find enough workers. The production manager at Baker Tools said that engineering firms are overbidding for labour and turnover is a constant problem for him. Both men gave the same reason – Aberdeen's acute housing shortage. 'When a man from Glasgow comes here,' said the Baker Tools manager, 'he's probably been made redundant and he's glad to get the job. But he's a skilled engineer and he thinks he's entitled to good living standards. When he finds that he hasn't a hope of a house or a flat in Aberdeen, he leaves.'

The waiting list for Council housing in Aberdeen District (which includes the suburbs) is over five thousand families. Councillor Bob Robertson, who was responsible for housing until local government reorganization, estimates that five thousand more haven't applied because they lack the necessary points. A couple sharing with parents haven't a chance unless they have children, and in that case they might get a flat in two years. It's thought, although no proper survey has been made, that about 1,500 men, women and children are living in caravan camps.

With the coming of the oil boom, the Council drew up a plan to build 3,500 homes each year from 1972 to 1976. The plan was conceived in a most un-Aberdonian spirit of visionary optimism, for there was never any likelihood of making it a reality, simply because the contractors had less than a third of the necessary labour force. The figures of completions make sad reading:

1970	1,690
1971	863
1972	91
1973	485
1974	154

This sorry performance had nothing to do with financial difficulties – for the 'oil capital', the Scottish Office guaranteed all the help it was asked for – nor with shortage of sites. It was purely a question of the shortage of building workers. There were not enough in the first place, and a vicious circle was set up – it was impossible to recruit more building workers because of the housing shortage. What made matters considerably worse was that most of the building workers theoretically available were, and still are, working on office blocks, hotels or private housing developments. Local government itself kicked into its own goal by embarking on a grandiose new City

Council housing estate, Aberdeen

Overleaf: Residential caravan site next to Shell headquarters, south fringe of Aberdeen. The centrally heated caravans cost about £2,300 in 1973 and double that by 1975

Council building, and a yet more grandiose head-quarters on the edge of the city for the Aberdeen-shire County Council (it is now the headquarters for the Grampian Region). Walking round Aberdeen, you see several big private office blocks under construction; one of them will have 78,000 square feet of floor space. As you might expect, one of the completed office blocks is empty.

'The Council could hardly find a contractor willing to tender,' said Robertson. 'The money's all in private building.' One not very prudent contract was for the Seaton Estate, a large develop-ment on the northern fringe of the city. It was a fixed-price contract, and when the work got behind schedule the expectations of profit were eroded by rising wages (once full employment reached Aberdeen) and inflation in general. The contracting company is now concentrating its efforts on private projects to offset its losses on the Seaton Estate. Out of 781 homes which ought to have been completed in 1972, only a few were finished when I took a look at this ill-fated venture in 1975.

It's fair to say that the outlook is improving. Office-building is tailing off, and there has been some increase in the labour force on housing. Councillor Charles Devine, now convenor of the housing committee, said that he reckoned on 900 completions in 1975 and a better figure in 1976.

Private house-building too has failed to make strides, perhaps because oil men making a fairly short stay prefer to rent flats – which they can find in older property – rather than to buy houses. Completions of houses for sale averaged 654 for the years 1967–71, before the oil boom, and 555 for the years 1972–74. Prices, for Aberdonians who are not in the oil business and do want to buy houses, have risen steeply. Average prices in north-eastern Scotland have trebled since 1970. They have trebled since 1970 in south-eastern

England too, and in the nation as a whole; but in most regions the big jump came in the earlier part of this period, whereas in north-eastern Scotland it has come in recent years, when the mortgage famine and inflation in other prices make things tougher for the new buyer. In the Grampian Region the average price for a three-bedroom semi-detached house in 1975 was £14,500, a little below London but higher than anywhere else in Britain. For a five-bedroom

detached house – a big house for a big oil man?
– it was £42,000, above even London's £40,000.
It had zoomed up from £31,000 between May and
November of 1974.

The traditional homes of the Aberdeen working-
class are called tenements, but don't resemble the
immense rambling tenement courts of Glasgow.
They stand along the streets and look at a glance
like individual houses; in fact they were built
to be divided into flats, usually four or six to a
building. The tenements were not slums, but the
flats are small and were built without separate
toilets or bathrooms. Many of them have been
taken over by the Council. The remaining private
owners do very well out of putting in bathrooms
and a veneer of modernization and selling the
flats. Often the buyers are young middle-class
people who want to live near the city centre
or near the university, and this accentuates the
housing shortage for the working-class. The
district secretary of the building trades union,
who knows Aberdeen thoroughly, told me that a
flat in an old tenement which could be bought
ten years ago for £500 now fetches £8,000.

Bob Middleton, who lives in a pleasant semi-
detached house in a fairly new development near
Aberdeen's ring road, bought it in 1970 for
£5,000. It would now fetch £15,000, so a man
earning Middleton's salary (he is a post office
engineer of senior status) wouldn't get a big
enough mortgage to meet the price, let alone a
younger man on an ordinary working-class wage.
A newly-built bungalow in a favoured village
along the coast can cost £24,000, a price which
reflects rocketing land values. While working-
class people can only wait for Council housing to
pick up, the middle classes have problems too.
A clergyman whose parish is in the most bourgeois
part of Aberdeen said sadly: 'Until a few years ago

a young couple giving notice of marriage would always let me know the new address, but now they don't.'

An estate agent's window gives the best insight into the situation. A one-bedroom top floor flat (admittedly in a charming old street) is priced at £6,500. A three-room flat 'suitable for bathroom conversion' – in other words, in an old building and without a bathroom or toilet – costs £2,500. A cottage in a village, on one floor, is £15,500. A modern house with seven acres of land is £35,000. This sounds like the best buy, for those in the right bracket.

As for short-term letting, rents sometimes have an element of the fantastic, and reached a dizzy height with the approach of the Offshore Oil Exhibition, held in September 1975. Aberdeen was expecting 20,000 visitors, some of them to be housed (if that's the word) on a cruise liner. The local paper carried an advertisement placed by three executives, who wanted a house or flat in Aberdeen or within an hour's reach, and offered £200 for five nights.

Councillor Devine showed me a letter, received by a Council tenant and written on the Housing Manager's notepaper, in which the bewildered recipient was asked to hand over his flat for the three weeks of the oil exhibition to 'Mr Abdur Ya-Marad and family'. He was offered hostel accommodation in Brechin – too far from Aberdeen for him to get to work – and an allowance of £5.30 a week for an adult, £2.65 for a child. The letter continued: 'Failure to comply with this request empowers me to requisition the accommodation for the stated period.' The notepaper was a photocopy, and a phone call to the Housing Manager established that the letter was a fake. The Housing Manager didn't sound much surprised; perhaps this wasn't a novelty to him.

£10,000 mobile cedarwood homes, fully furnished and centrally heated, within a mile of the Petroleum Club. 100 such homes are planned for the site

No one – certainly no one in the Labour movement of Aberdeen – would wish either to deny or to forfeit the benefits that the oil rush has brought, primarily in jobs and wages. But there are other entries in the balance-sheet: the housing shortage and its attendant rackets, the uncertainties and the planlessness, the harsh and dangerous life on the rigs . . . 'poor working conditions, poor living conditions, and a general reduction in the quality of life'. In Aberdeen, one cannot think of North Sea oil solely in terms of a balance of payments surplus.

Private speculative building outside Aberdeen

BOOM TOWN

'You've got to go to Peterhead,' they all say in Aberdeen, 'if you want to see what the impact of the oil boom really means.' In absolute terms – one could compare the investment figures, the scale of construction in harbour improvement and building supply bases, the traffic now plying from those bases to the rigs – the impact on each town has been similar. But in Aberdeen it was happening to a city of 185,000 people, already a regional centre in the style of Bristol or Norwich. In Peterhead it was happening to a town of 14,000, and an exceptionally inward-looking town at that. Nothing much had changed in Peterhead for decades, and those who dominated local life – a staid, conservative group of solid citizens and 'independent' Councillors – didn't want any change. 'They had built a wall round the town,' says Ian Hutcheson, who manages the British Legion club, 'and the oil companies broke down the wall. So the place exploded.'

Before the oil rush, anyone who had heard of Peterhead connected it with the maximum security prison, a formidable structure on a windswept hill outside the town, and with fishing. It was never on anyone's tourist itinerary, but it's a handsome town in an austere fashion. Everything is built in red granite – you notice the cottages change from grey to red as you drive the thirty miles from Aberdeen. The main streets are broad and dignified, and the one actually called Broad Street is in fact a square of pleasing proportions. The bay, which had a beach until the oil supply-boats came, makes a noble curve between two headlands. Sunbathing on the beach was rare, however, for Peterhead people admit (or sometimes claim with pride) that this corner of

Peterhead harbour

Scotland has the foulest weather in the British Isles. When there isn't a storm, one of them said resignedly, there's a fog. In the long winter, it is bitterly cold. It doesn't often snow in the town, but the roads over the Buchan hills are often blocked, which helps to account for Peterhead's insularity.

Most of the Peterhead fishing-boats are small, and go out by the day to fish the inshore waters. A boat is owned jointly by its crew of five, often members of a family, and when the catch is sold each man gets a share. Until about ten years ago there was little industrial employment, except in small ship-repair yards and in the Crosse and Black-

well factory, which makes fish-paste, employs mainly women, and has paid low wages. Many young men, especially those who had done well at the Peterhead Academy, left the town to find work in Aberdeen or in more distant places. Despite the exodus, unemployment was at 7% in the 1950s.

The 1960s saw an economic upturn. Three new factories came to the town: one making gear-boxes which was taken over by General Motors, another engineering works owned by the Cleveland Twist Drill Co., and a textile mill. Fishing enjoyed a remarkable boom, partly because some larger trawlers started to use Peterhead, a non-

Peterhead: new fishmarket

union port, instead of Aberdeen where the catch is unloaded by porters belonging to trade unions. Fish sales at Peterhead rose from a value of under £1 million in 1970 to nearly £10 million in the peak year, 1973. As the crews of the larger trawlers were Aberdeen men, this didn't provide any extra jobs, but good inshore catches meant that a member of a Peterhead crew could take home £100 a week.

These developments, however, don't seem to have inspired Peterhead with a spirit of optimism. Young men continued to go south; people who made money were not generally inclined to buy houses or consumer goods. Employment fluctuated as nation-wide recessions affected the factories. And the fishing boom was distrusted – rightly, as it has turned out – as a mere interruption to a long-term decline.

The one durable benefit was the improvement of the harbour: that is, not the small fishing harbour at the bottom of Broad Street, but the bay. This had been designated back in 1886 as a Harbour of Refuge; the idea was that storm-damaged ships from all over the North Sea would make for Peterhead, each bringing work to the repair yards. One stone jetty was built by prison labour in the nineteenth century. But two jetties are needed to keep rough seas out of a harbour, and the Peterhead Harbour Trust – not very keen to welcome strangers, perhaps – didn't get the other one built until 1958, and then didn't make it high enough. When the oil rush began, however, the mere existence of this ample harbour proved to be a mighty piece of good luck for Peterhead. A glance was enough to show that it was an ideal situation for supply bases. Nowadays, the bay is always busy with supply-boats. Not only this, but when the winter storms set in rigs are towed to Peterhead for overhaul or repair.

On the southern shore of the bay, just below the hill on which the prison stands, a base has been set up by the Aberdeen Service Company. The height of the jetty has been increased, and a Dutch reclamation company was called in to make a stretch of level ground. The base was in business by early 1974; the warehouses were ready a year ahead of schedule; and an engineering workshop is to be the next development. The base is used

Peterhead harbour

Opposite : Aberdeen Service Company supply base

by eighty ships a week in summer and thirty a week in winter. Ian Currall, the manager, was careful to stress to me that all his employees are Peterhead men, and that they are kept on the payroll in winter although the work slackens off. There are two hundred jobs.

Across the bay, on a hitherto deserted peninsula called Keith Inch, another base has been built and now belongs to the British Oxygen Company. (This is an example of diversified investment; no oxygen is made at Keith Inch.) BOC employs 170 people – nine tenths of them are natives of Peterhead, I was told – but other companies using the base provide more jobs at various times. The Keith Inch base is the largest anywhere along the North Sea coast, with long quays and an enormous warehouse. As well as servicing the rigs, it sends out supplies to the pipe-laying barges. It handles twenty ships a day in summer and about four a day in winter, when pipe-laying work is drastically reduced.

Aberdeen Service Company supply base

More. The pipeline from the Forties oilfield, through which Britain's first major quantities of oil began to flow in November 1975, reaches the coast at Cruden Bay, between Peterhead and Aberdeen. Peterhead was the base for the undersea pipelaying, and Peterhead men found work as welders and labourers on the underground part of the line.

More. A big power station – a £100 million project, among the largest in Scotland – is being built at Boddam, three miles south of Peterhead. The construction work is being done by 1,200 men brought by the contractors and living in a workcamp, but when the power station goes into operation in 1978 it will provide many jobs for electricians and others.

More. The power station will run on oil, brought by tankers. (The oil coming through the pipeline is destined for refineries.) It will need 6,500 tons of oil a day, which means a lot of tankers. They will be moored and serviced at a tanker terminal, yet to be built, in Peterhead Bay.

More. Natural gas, from the rich Frigg gasfield in the Norwegian sector of the North Sea, is to be brought through a pipeline coming ashore at St Fergus, two miles north of Peterhead. This pipeline is still under construction. From St Fergus the gas will be distributed to many parts of Scotland, and this involves the building of a big gas terminal.

More. There are plans for building an ammonia plant close to the St Fergus terminal and using the gas.

More. If Aberdeen is the oil capital, Peterhead is at least a secondary centre. Some oil companies have branch offices; some drilling companies, supply-boats and pipe construction companies work from Peterhead. This has created a local demand for white-collar workers, something

Keith Inch supply base

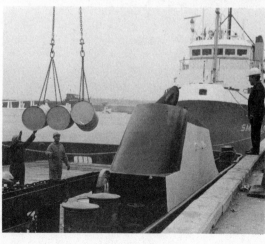

McClelland
engineers, ltd.
◆ geotechnical
consultants,

LONG VEHICLE

almost unprecedented in Peterhead's history. At
the Academy, many more girls are taking commercial courses – 'the oil firms are screaming for
secretaries,' said a teacher – and it has become
popular to take Higher Certificate in economics,
followed by a degree in business studies which is
now available from a college in Aberdeen. The
result of all these developments is that – as
Ian Hutcheson, who doesn't approve of the oil
rush, put it – 'the labour market has been upset.'
He told me about a young woman who applied
for a job as a typist with an American company.
Having accepted her, the manager said: 'We'll pay
you twelve.' The girl said she'd been hoping for
fifteen. 'OK, fifteen,' the manager agreed. Only
after starting work did she discover that she was
getting £1,500 a year, not £15 a week.

It was the labour market that had always
governed wages in Peterhead, for trade unionism
had been weak except in the two engineering
plants. In industrial towns where the unions are
strongly entrenched, wage-rates continue to be
reasonable even in periods of unemployment; but

New roads have to be
built to carry the huge
loads

Top: Peterhead street
Above: Five years ago
Don Mackay was
earning £550 p.a. in a
local factory. In 1975 he
was earning £3500 as
personnel manager at the
Brown & Root base

here the sudden arrival of full employment, and indeed labour shortages, made a dramatic difference. George Baird, a Labour Councillor who is a disabled man, told me that six years ago he had been working in a ship-chandler's store for £13 a week. Now, as a storeman at the gas terminal, he earns £75. 'And that's because I'm disabled – most of the men earn £100.' Building workers can earn £100 for a 56-hour week. Workers at the supply bases get a basic £40, which they can be sure of in winter when there's not much to keep them busy, and make £100 or more with overtime in summer. Even the wages for labourers on the roads jumped from £22 to £43 within two years. All employers, including Crosse and Blackwell, have had to raise wages at least to national standards. It must be remembered, too, that living in Peterhead is fairly cheap. Few people need to pay fares to get to work. Council rents have risen, but rates are low, and families in some older houses belonging to small landlords pay a rent of only one pound a week.

The other side of the coin – as in Aberdeen – is a

serious housing shortage, accentuated by the return of many people who had left Peterhead. The Rev. James Alexander, who had been convenor of the housing committee before the Town Council was absorbed by the Buchan District Council, gave me the facts. In the old quiet days the Council's building record had been adequate and there was no real housing need. In May 1971, soon after the announcement of the Forties oil strike, Mr Alexander urged the Council to buy land and start some new schemes. But he failed to convince the majority of the Councillors, who didn't believe that the oil rush would ever happen (or didn't want it to touch Peterhead). It did happen, and the waiting list shot up from fifty to six hundred – one important factor, Mr Alexander says, was that better wages meant younger marriages. Land prices shot up too, and in 1974 the Council found itself paying £16,000 an acre to acquire a caravan site which could have been bought, when Mr Alexander made his rejected proposals, for £2,000 an acre. This means that Peterhead now has no residential caravan site, which could be useful while so many people are waiting for houses. There has been difficulty in finding building sites within the town. The Scottish Special Housing Association, which is supposed to build houses in places where they are urgently needed and particularly in centres of the oil boom, owned a large site for six years and never laid a brick. Meanwhile the Council had completed only 70 houses or flats, in small 'gap schemes', between 1971 and my visit to Peterhead in 1975.

However, things are now moving, with 180 houses under construction, and work due to begin in 1976 on 300 more on what was formerly the prison farm. There seems to be no labour problem; the contractor is an English firm and, while employing some local labour, has also brought in workers living in a camp. The SSHA is at last getting busy with a scheme for 400 homes, and another 400 are to be built by the District Council on land not far outside the town boundary.

New private houses are starting to go up at a good rate, adding a straggle to the hitherto compact town. A large international company has started a development of 400 houses, and a local firm is building 100. Some people build their own homes. Having paid for the plot and £1,000 for services, you can buy a timber-frame for £3,000 and pay a builder £1,000 to assemble it. You add the walls and the roof yourself, or it will be done by someone working on his own account by personal arrangement, known in Scotland as a 'homer'. The cost of buying a house has risen sharply, as an estate agent made clear to me. A bungalow, bought in 1973 for £11,500, is being resold for £15,000. An old granite house in one of the better streets may fetch £20,000. About twenty houses have been bought by companies – Total Oil and British Gas – but in general the oil companies are more interested in renting; a one-bedroom flat can cost £150 a month. The estate agent gave me an interesting example of how localized the oil boom is. He was selling two almost identical houses, one in Peterhead for £15,000 and one in Buckie, where there are no oil developments, for £8,000.

There are people in Peterhead who deplore the oil boom, sometimes out of sheer conservatism and nostalgia for the placid little town which they no longer recognize, sometimes because they don't like paying higher wages to a shop assistant or a daily help, but sometimes for other reasons. There is concern about changes in the social atmosphere, of which I shall have more to say.

Speculation

Left: Opposite
Peterhead maximum
security gaol

There is anxiety about pollution from the tanker
terminal and the ammonia plant. And oil is bad
news for owners and skippers of fishing boats.
The oil boom coincided with – and has partly
caused – a sudden collapse of the fishing boom.

A skipper named Adam Stewart told me that
1975 had been the worst year he could remember.
Over the three summer months the men in his
crew had been living on an average of £20 a week,
although a spell when the boat was under repair
was one reason for this depressing figure. Fishing,
in fact, is once again a chancy livelihood, as it
has been for most of Scotland's history. The
catches are poor, and undoubtedly this is nature's
revenge for the over-fishing of the North Sea.
What's new since 1973 is the high cost of fuel and
– because of the new level of wages in Peterhead –
the high cost of repairs. Besides, crews are leaving
the trawlers to work on the supply-boats, or

The high cost of repairs is making fishing uneconomical. Many fishing boats have been damaged by oil-related debris

Above: Supply boats find it easier to pay the cost of repairs

Above right: Fishermen claim that fish choke on disposable mugs dumped from supply boats, rigs, etc.

else to stay on shore and take the jobs now available. Good steady wages look like a better bargain than the now problematical share of the catch. 'The only ones who'll stay are the men for whom fishing is a way of life,' Stewart said. 'There's not many young ones among them, and there'll be fewer. Most of the boats will soon be up for sale, I expect. Oil has killed fishing, that's the truth of it.' But hasn't oil been good for Peterhead on the whole? 'It's been good for the poor families,' Stewart conceded. Through this phrase, one has an insight into an upheaval in the gradations of Peterhead society. Under the old system the fishing crews were an elite; they didn't always make money but they were the only working-class people who ever did, while men dependent on labouring jobs ashore were 'the poor'. Now it looks like being the other way round.

But a bank manager, in a good position to take an overall view, is in no doubt that the oil boom is 'a massive boost to the economy'. Small engineering and haulage firms are thriving, he says, charging whatever they please because their customers are always in a hurry. Individual and family savings show a big increase; Peterhead people tend to save, both because it's traditional and because they are wary that the good times may be brief. Even so, they are buying houses, buying cars, buying consumer durables of every kind.

If it's true that you could visit Aberdeen without being struck by signs of the oil boom, it's impossible to take a quick walk round Peterhead without being aware of a new prosperity. Shops display expensive cameras, expensive record-players and hi-fi equipment, expensive golf-clubs and fishing-rods. One large window is crammed with records, tapes and cassettes. There are four new male boutiques, one with the significant name of Black Gold, selling frilly shirts, patterned shirts and ties, scarlet and bottle-green and sky-blue jackets, T-shirts decorated with helicopters and other symbols of the oil rush. An old-established men's outfitter, still relying on his tweed suits and caps, says that the new competition doesn't worry him and his turnover has doubled in the last couple of years. Women don't do so well; it seems that their men don't like them to take up the latest fashions, and boutiques for girls in the main streets have failed. However, toward the edge of town I notice two boutiques called Mod Corner and Shangri-La.

Two old and until recently ailing hotels, the Caledonian and the Royal (all Scots towns have hotels called the Caledonian and the Royal) have taken on a new lease of life. All rooms are always full. The comfortable lounge bar of the Caledonian is where people who matter in the oil world meet; the bars of the Royal, as crowded as wartime pubs, are for the 'other ranks'. Ron Ferrari, a native of Peterhead despite his name, presides genially over

Spanish barge workers on a shopping spree in Peterhead

Male boutique: names like Rigg and Black Gold are conspicuous

the Caledonian bar. A few years ago he owned nothing but a strategically placed fish-and-chip shop; when you ask the way you're usually told to turn right, or left, at Ferrari's fish shop. He saw the oil rush coming, and now he owns the Caledonian, the Royal, and – it's said – half the main street. If he isn't a millionaire, everyone in Peterhead thinks he is.

Everyone who has anything to sell is doing well – the clothing shops, the jeweller, the shop with fine briar pipes. One might suppose that the big buyers are the incomers and the transient oil men. But shopkeepers all say that their customers are mainly local people.

'I'm staggered by what's happened to the old place,' says a man who is back after emigrating to Australia in the bleak 1950s. Yet what has hit the old place isn't so much a transformation – for in many ways Peterhead retains its character – as an unassimilated surprise; you could call Peterhead the town that won the pools. The staid, solid granite houses wear an air of bewilderment. Black Gold, the Granada Lounge and Wong's Chinese restaurant have arrived, but the British Legion club and the Seamen's Mission Hall remain.

If incongruity is the dominant chord (or dis-

Above: Ron Ferrari has made a fortune from the oil boom

Above: The Royal,
Peterhead

Below: The Caledonian
Hotel, Peterhead

cord), it's mainly because the centre of town is
more full of strangers than Leicester Square at the
height of the tourist season: strangers from other
parts of Britain and from all over the world.
There's no country club for the oil executives and
managers, no American colony with its self-
enclosed life. At a working-class level, there's no
dockside quarter. The men from a Norwegian
tug, or a Greek freighter in port to transfer
Japanese steel for the pipeline, converge on the
Royal. The workers on the pipe-laying barge,
close inshore while I was in Peterhead, are mainly
Italians.

In Marischal Street two Texans in their ten-
gallon hats stand with hands in their ornamented
belts, looking like the sheriff and the owner of
Red Creek Ranch in an old movie. Outside the
supermarket a Cockney Mum – up to visit her
son, I suppose – is saying: 'Well, I don't know, it's
not the same, is it?' A Welsh ship's engineer greets
me and I remember him from a couple of nights
ago. In the Caledonian bar an American is
telling an Australian friend about his phone call to
his wife: 'She says, here I am stuck with the kids
while you're living it up in Peterhead. I tell her,
honey, if that's what you think you better come to

Peterhead.' At Wong's, the foursome at the next
table are speaking polished French; by their
features, one of the men and one of the stylishly
dressed women must be Vietnamese. In the
Granada Lounge, I wait to buy a drink behind
two very tall and very handsome blacks, their
long legs encased in wranglers. They're speaking a
language I can't quite identify over the surrounding noise. It could be Portuguese and they could
be from Angola, or maybe Guinea-Bissau. Anything is possible in Peterhead.

The Granada Lounge is fantastic. Once a pub
like any other pub, it appears to have been taken
over by an entrepreneur who, in true Peterhead
style, began with an ice-cream shop. The building
was re-faced to exclude any possibility of daylight
filtering in, and the upper floor redesigned in what
might be called Spanish package-holiday style.
Part of the roof is made of dark-blue perspex,
and two half-obscured floodlights help to replace
the clouded skies of Scotland by a semblance of a
balmy Mediterranean night. This pseudo-heaven

**The Granada,
Peterhead**

is fringed by red tiles suggesting a Spanish court-yard. There are tables and plastic bench-seats, there is a long bar, and there's a tiny dance-floor, reasonably adequate since men outnumber women by ten to one. The doors to the toilets are labelled Senores and Senoritas. A pop group plays ener-getically while customers try to make themselves heard in all the languages and dialects of Peter-head, but often in Italian because the Granada is much favoured by the pipe-laying men. The place is packed every night. In this strident and garish atmosphere it's difficult to believe that you're in the middle of a small, secluded and conservative Scottish town. That, presumably, is why the Granada is packed.

But the Granada – or the Caledonian, or the Royal – is no place for the teenager still at school, hoping to enter the oil world in a serious way by taking his Higher Cert in economics or geology, and meanwhile outside the magic circle of high earnings and free spending. There are no coffee-bars, nowhere to sit and chat over a coke if you're

**The Granada,
Peterhead**

below drinking age, nowhere to get anything to
eat in the evening except a full dinner. The few
halls belong to the churches, of denominations
ranging from the official Presbyterian to others
more rigorously opposed to the pursuit of enjoy-
ment. Dances and other light-hearted social
activities are rare. For the native-born young
generation, Peterhead is still Dullsville. An intelligent girl, spending the summer with her parents,
said that she couldn't wait to get back to Aberdeen
University. For that matter, there's nothing for the
middle-aged person who in a more lively town
would be in the amateur dramatic society or taking
up pottery, nor for the sociably inclined pensioner.

The idea of a community centre has been under
discussion since 1963. A stranger might think
that the disused church, right in the middle of

town at the top of Broad Street, would do nicely; a similar church is a flourishing Arts Centre in Aberdeen. But Peterhead isn't inclined to take provisional measures, and is waiting for the big new community centre which is at last being built with funds from Grampian Region, on a site which will also have a new building for the Academy. By all accounts it will be a magnificent place, with a sports hall, a swimming-pool, a theatre, and rooms for meetings and classes. It will be rather far from the town centre, and even farther from the new housing estates, and some people are afraid that young people won't patronize it because of its association with the school; still, Peterhead will have a community centre. One can't say that the project has been pushed ahead with the same urgency as a supply base or a gas terminal. It should be ready in 1978.

Meanwhile, there are no youth clubs except a few run by the churches and attracting the more obedient children of church members. Bobby Simmers, the jeweller in Chapel Street, is much concerned about this situation and says that Peterhead people who might act as club leaders lack a sense of responsibility to the community. He is the main figure in the Boy Scouts; he points out that five of the eight scoutmasters are incomers, and the Boys' Brigade has collapsed for want of adult help. 'So what do you get? Naturally, a lot of under-age drinking. The lads buy a bottle in the afternoon and drink it out in the street, or else at home in the evening. Dad's in the pub and Mum's playing bingo.'

Most of the trouble in Peterhead, in the form of fights or disturbances, involves local youngsters at a frustrating loose end. There's more trouble than in most Scots towns, policemen who have worked elsewhere say. The foreigners are not blamed – 'you couldn't find a nicer lot than these

Peterhead

Italians,' Simmers says. Another explanation is that the pipe-laying workers would be arbitrarily sacked if they misbehaved. Naturally, however, the young men of Peterhead don't feel very friendly toward the Italians who can offer the girls a lively evening at the Granada. Ian Hutcheson, with his

gift for the evocative phrase, says: 'There is great rivalry between the local swains and the incoming gallants.' On one occasion, the swains gathered by the harbour to throw stones and bricks at a boat taking Italians back to their barge.

Crime in Peterhead is mostly theft or housebreaking. Those responsible are sometimes local men, sometimes incomers (British, not foreign) who came to look for work and haven't found it yet. Serious violence is rare, although two men in the past year have been charged with attempted murder. Sudden deaths are accidental; two or three times a year someone falls into the harbour while returning to a ship and is drowned, whether because of a sudden gust of wind or a rapid intake of whisky. Despite the large numbers of men around the place without their womenfolk, there are no recorded cases of rape or indecent assault. When I expressed surprise, I was told: 'Our whores do a valuable job.'

The Peterhead whores – not many of them – are established figures in the community, rather like prostitutes in a Maupassant story, and known by name to many perfectly respectable citizens. Their efforts are supplemented, of course, by a certain number of more amateur good time girls. Nevertheless, Peterhead husbands worry about their wives yielding to seduction by Italian charm or American money. There are in fact recurrent scandals, and more divorces than Peterhead was ever used to. 'I wouldn't take my wife into a pub where she'd be pestered by a Yank,' one man says emphatically. One has to remember that until fairly recently a small-town Scot wouldn't take his wife into a pub at all, and this tradition is only gradually being eroded as the old hard-drinking bars turn into neighbourhood meeting-places in the English fashion. I heard the view expressed that, if a wife takes up with an American, it's because her husband hasn't been out for an evening with her or bought her a nice dress, or indeed listened to what she says, for years.

It's hard for the visitor to estimate how much Peterhead has changed underneath the surface glitter. But it's unlikely that most people would be willing to go back to the old static society, the accepted hierarchies, the wall round the town – or the low wages and limited opportunities. The question one doesn't like to think about is what happens if the oil boom doesn't last. No one has thought much about attracting other types of industry to the town; as one trade unionist said to me gloomily, it could be back to 7% unemployment pretty quickly.

Meanwhile, Peterhead is the most extraordinary town in Britain. It isn't, though one hopes that it may become, a place of settled prosperity. It is what one has read about in history, and didn't expect to see in this improbable setting between the mountains and the cold grey sea – in every sense of the phrase, a boom town.

Peterhead

THE LAST FRONTIER

The Shetland Isles are the last frontier of the oil boom, unless and until it veers round to the Outer Hebrides. Some of the richest oilfields lie in these northerly latitudes, and the oil will be brought to the Shetlands in at least two pipelines, perhaps ultimately six. There it will be trans-shipped or possibly refined, though the building of a refinery is far from a certainty. Anyway, if the boom comes up to expectations, the amount of oil 'belonging' to the Shetlands in the 1980s may equal the amount produced in Kuwait. As there are only 19,000 Shetlanders, whereas Kuwait has a population of 750,000, the sheikhdom would be handsomely surpassed in income per capita. It wouldn't astonish me to see the Shetlands set up as an independent state; Mr Jo Grimond, the permanent MP since 1950, would make an admirable President.

A hundred and twenty miles of sea, with the Orkneys and Fair Isle in between, divide the Shetlands from the nearest point on the Scottish mainland. The largest island, confusingly known as Mainland, is 72 miles long but in most places only half a dozen miles across. There are fifty other islands, or seventy, or a hundred – it depends on whom you ask, and on the distinction between an island and a rock. Shetlanders enjoy telling you that, confronted with a bureaucratic form in which one of the questions was 'Nearest railway station', they put 'Bergen'. A glance at an atlas shows that the station at Wick is considerably nearer than Bergen, but the anecdote tells you how the Shetlanders look at the world. They are of

Construction wharf at
Shell's pipeline terminal,
Sullom Voe, Shetland

Norse descent and have a language akin to
Norwegian, although it's used mainly in mottoes
and inscriptions. They don't like their islands to
be regarded as a part of Scotland. The Scottish
National Party managed to get 17% of the vote
in the last election for the Orkney and Shetland
constituency – mainly in the Orkneys, Shetlanders
declare – but majority feeling is not moving in this
direction; most Shetlanders say that they would
rather deal with Englishmen, Norwegians or

Shell construction site at Sullom Voe, with crofts in the background

Americans, or for that matter practically anybody, than with 'mainland' Scots. With devolution in the air, the Shetland Council has passed a resolution laying down that 'in the event of constitutional change our links should be with Westminster rather than Edinburgh'. One wonders if it has occurred to English politicians, faced with Scottish nationalism, to play the Shetland card.

When Scottish local government was reorganized, the Shetlanders were threatened with being included in the vast Highland Region, which stretches from quite near Glasgow to John o'Groats. As a result of anxious representations, Parliament gave autonomous status to the Shetlands, as well as to the Orkneys and the Hebrides. The Shetland Council was given extensive planning and financial powers in what's called the Shetland Act, which is greatly cherished and considered as a charter of liberty, rather like the 'British North America Act' which was the cornerstone of Canadian nationhood. One consequence was that these outposts were separately counted in the EEC referendum, when the Shetlands and the Hebrides were unique in producing a 'No' majority. As a matter of fact, Shetlanders were somewhat embarrassed by coming up with a result pleasing to the SNP and displeasing to Mr Grimond, and one Councillor earnestly explained to me that it happened only because it was

Shell pipeline coming
ashore at Firth Voe

raining and the townspeople – who include some 'mainland' Scots – voted more heavily than the crofters.

Coming by air from Aberdeen, you land at Sumburgh, on the southerly tip of the main island, and find that you are twenty-six miles from Lerwick, the only town. (Lerwick is therefore farther from its airport than London, Paris or New York.) The road is narrow and winding, and was sign-posted as A970 only a few years ago; before that, Shetlanders didn't bother about A and B roads. Cars are outnumbered by taxis, which have quadrupled since 'the oil' came and do a roaring trade. Shetlanders don't usually travel far from their homes, and travellers between Sumburgh and Lerwick are mostly connected with 'the oil'; they are here for anything between a day and a few months and are unlikely to have imported their cars. A drive-on-drive-off ferry is planned but not yet in existence.

It is, of course, light nearly all the time in summer and dark nearly all the time in winter. The predominant colour of sky and sea is grey. The predominant atmosphere is damp and chilly. The fine summer of 1975, when it was possible to sit out of doors without a coat, was a rare experience for Shetlanders. The last time this had happened was in 1947, an old lady told me with precision.

The drive to Lerwick gives you a fair idea of Shetland scenery, though it doesn't take you to the more remote spots. Between one rocky coast and the other, there is practically no level ground. The hills are not very high, but you have the feeling of travelling among formidable mountains. Very little of the land is cultivated; you see tiny hayfields and vegetable plots in a few sheltered corners, but most of the scattered crofts depend on sheep-farming – Shetlanders don't live in villages, except round fishing harbours. There are no trees, no hedges, no gorse or bracken or heather, only turf broken here and there by grey boulders, so that – unless you've been this far north before – your associations are with the highest ranges of, for instance, the Alps. The rare trees of the Shetlands have been deliberately planted and are notable landmarks; 'I'll meet you at the tree' is a traditional joke. One's thoughts tend naturally to what it would be like to be lost in the hills, especially when they're mysteriously shrouded in drizzling rain or swirling mist, as they are most of the time.

Lerwick has a population of 6,000 and two main streets. The Esplanade is nobly named but miniscule in scale; it faces the harbour, it's about two hundred yards long, and the main buildings are the Harbour Trust office and the fish-market. Parked cars and narrow pavements, to say nothing of the weather, discourage strolling. The place for this is Commercial Street, where the shops are. It is stone-paved and of irregular width, so everyone walks down the middle and it's avoided by cars, except vans making deliveries to the shops. Since the oil boom, which has multiplied the number of cars and taxis in Lerwick, thought has been given to closing Commercial Street officially to traffic. But 'No Entry' signs, like A and B roads, are a 'mainland' idea.

These streets are criss-crossed by narrow alleys and by little streets with steps, so Lerwick is decidedly picturesque. Clambering up the steps to get a view of the harbour and the cliffs beyond, on an August morning when the sun made a brief appearance, I made comparisons with coastal towns in Wales and Cornwall, even in the Mediterranean. The reflection induced thoughts of souvenir shops, craft shops, antique shops, ice-cream and sandwich shops, tea-shops, pubs and bars with awnings – hopefully, good sea-food restaurants. But Lerwick has none of these, any more than it has ten-storey hotels with balconies, or camping and caravan sites, or two-hour trips round the bay. Despite its charm and character (or, perhaps, to retain its charm and character) Lerwick has virtually no tourists. This comment from me amazed a resident, who said: 'But this year we're simply overrun with tourists.' Spending the day in and around the town on foot, I counted six. (They were easily identified by their air of bewilderment and their hand-knitted Shetland sweaters.) There is one restaurant, which had just opened.

It isn't easy to get to the Shetlands, since the boats only run twice a week and the air services are frequently halted by fogs. And it has been rendered more difficult, paradoxically, by the oil boom. Seats on the planes are heavily booked by oil companies, drilling companies and construction companies (these seats, of course, are not always used). When I tried, on a Thursday, to get an interview with the Chief Executive of the Shetland Council, I was told: 'He's been trying to get back from the mainland since Monday.' Since the little airport also has to deal with rig-workers travelling in charter planes, or desperately trying to get home after being landed from the rigs by helicopter, it has the atmosphere of a refugee camp. The oil

Overleaf: Waiting for the plane to Lerwick, hours late

companies also book almost all the hotel rooms
and pay for them whether they're needed or not.
Not having planned in advance to go to the
Shetlands at all – we were offered a visit to the
Conoco rig at short notice – we were very lucky
to be able to stay with friends. Even the youth
hostel, I gathered, is booked up months in advance.

'Happy is the land that has no history,' said
Brecht, and the Shetlands haven't had much. The
events mainly recalled are visitations by strangers
from the world to the south: that is, the two world
wars when the strangers were in Navy or Air
Force uniform and, on a more startling scale, the
oil rush. However, the Shetlands have not been
entirely happy. It has always been difficult to make
a living, and for decades young men have left
the islands to seek work in Scotland or England,
or have emigrated (generally to Canada), or have
joined the Merchant Marine. Shetlanders divide
sharply into those who have seen nothing of the
wider world, and those who have seen much more
of it than the average Londoner. The population,
now 19,000, had touched a low of 17,000 just
before the oil boom.

'The oil', in fact, is something of a rescue
operation for the Shetlands. The two traditional
mainstays of the economy – fishing and hand-
knitted wool – are both in a critical state. Fishing,
as we have seen, is doing badly everywhere, and
the knitters have for some reason lost important
export markets.

The new prosperity is still in its early stages,
because the oil strikes off the Shetlands were made
later than those off Aberdeen. Rumours and hopes
came quicker than realities. One Shetlander said
to me: 'It's not happening the way we expected
in 1972. It's all *mañana*, really. We're beginning
to ask, when does the boom begin? There's
politics involved, don't you think so?' There's also

a suspicion that when the boom does start it will be short-lived, because most of the jobs will be on construction projects. Sullom Voe, a sheltered inlet toward the northern end of the main island (the word 'voe' is cognate with 'fjord'), has been chosen as the terminal for the pipelines, and construction here will provide 1,200 jobs when it's at its peak – when we were in the Shetlands, it had just got under way. Two service bases, supplying material to the rigs and to the pipe-laying barges, have been created near Lerwick; harbour improvements at Lerwick, and the drive-on ferry for cars and lorries, are other important projects; and the airport runway at Sumburgh is being extended. But some of the work, especially at remote Sullom Voe, will be done by men brought from the mainland by contractors and living in camps.

However, there ought to be a substantial number of permanent jobs, in proportion to the small population of the Shetlands. The Lerwick bases have brought eighty jobs so far. Sullom Voe will offer at least a hundred, and many more if a refinery is built there. There are jobs at the airport, jobs in hotels now busy all year round, jobs driving taxis, and above all jobs building houses. The Council has built 1,200 houses within the last three years, but there's still a two-year waiting list and more will be needed. A fair amount of building is also being done for the private market, including some by 'homers'. Wages are not tremendous when compared with those being earned in other parts of the oil scene, but a service-base job with overtime can bring in £80.

As well as this, the new industry has been of benefit to small businesses – to light engineering workshops, to garages, to transport contractors. The big companies can't bring their equipment or their repair services to these islands so easily as to a mainland town, so they make deals with local firms, even with local mechanics and drivers working as self-employed freelances. It's not unusual for a Shetlander, who not long ago had only his croft to give him a livelihood, to invest in a bulldozer and hire it by the day – perhaps driving it himself – to a construction project. So money is finding its way to homes all over the islands. One of the banks has increased its staff from twelve to twenty-six, mainly to meet the need for mobile units visiting remote places one day a week. And there alone, by the way, are fourteen new jobs.

But the wealth of the Shetlands, as a community, has been increased principally thanks to the determined policies of the Council. At the outset of the boom, a development company managed to buy land at Sandwick, halfway between Sumburgh and Lerwick, and get a service base built before anyone had noticed. The Chief Executive felt that such things mustn't happen again, especially as Sandwick wasn't a place where development was considered suitable. Asking around, Councillors discovered that developers and land speculators were buying land from innocent crofters all over the Shetlands. One company had got a firm grip on Sullom Voe, the proposed site of the pipeline terminals. In general, there was a distinct possibility of development in all the wrong places: places where there was no housing and the Council would be obliged to provide it, places where nobody needed work, places of great natural beauty, places where the wild life had to be protected. The Shetlands can boast of several kinds of rare birds, such as the snowy owl, and also rare plants. But the ecological balance is delicate, and rough handling could irrevocably destroy it.

The Shetlands had never had, nor seemed to need, a planning department, but clearly it was high time to set one up, and it came into existence – with a devoted staff of three – in September 1973.

Russian dumper truck. German excavators and much other foreign equipment is being used at Sullom Voe, as British equipment is unavailable

The first necessity was to get control of Sullom Voe, and this was done by stalling on planning permission until the development company saw that it wouldn't get a free hand. Eventually the Council acquired the land there, partly by compulsory purchase. The land around the airport was acquired too, and the coastal land in and near Lerwick belongs to the Harbour Trust, a public body, so all the nerve-centres of the oil boom are now in the control of the community.

The ground rents charged to base operators and developers are pretty steep, and it seems that the Arabs have nothing on the Shetlanders when it comes to ensuring that the money from oil stays where it's made. The increased 'national income' is to be spent on the needs of the community – for instance, on a sports centre for Lerwick, which at present has very scanty facilities for leisure and recreation. The Council also intends to keep life relatively cheap for the islanders. Because of transport costs, a Council house that

could be built on the mainland for £13,000 demands £20,000 in the Shetlands. Nevertheless, rents and rates are the lowest in the United Kingdom. A three-bedroom house is rented for £132 a year, plus £30 rates.

Planning also means that development will be limited to three areas – Sullom Voe, Lerwick and Sumburgh – leaving the rest of the Shetlands to the crofters and the snowy owls. Local plans have been commissioned from major consultants such as Llewellyn Davies. The guiding idea is that the coming changes should be less than a total transformation. At Sullom Voe, where there are four small villages, the planners considered the creation of a new town, but decided to enlarge the villages and preserve their distinct identities.

Significantly – and in this respect following the Norwegian strategy – the Shetland planners want to restrain the pace of the oil rush. If some people feel that the boom isn't coming so fast as they expected, the answer is that this is all to the good.

Construction of work camp for 1200 Sullom Voe workers. Meanwhile construction workers have to live in mobile homes

CHARGES for DAMAGE or LOSS to ACCOMMODATION FURNISHINGS.

ITEMS.	COST OF REPLACEMENT PER ITEM.	
	£	p.
BED	15	00
MATTRESS	10	00
HEAD BOARD	4	00
WALL BOARD	6	00
BEDSIDE CABINET	13	50
DRESSING UNIT	52	00
UPRIGHT CHAIR	10	50
SHEET	2	00
PILLOWCASE	1	25
FEATHER PILLOW	1	50
BOLSTER PILLOW	2	70
BLANKET		70
WASTE BIN		80
ASHTRAY		30
COATHANGER		10
BEDSPREAD	7	50
HAND TOWEL	2	50
TOWEL RING	1	50
CURTAIN (LINED)	11	00

Grand Met (who also cater for Kishorn site) say that no expense is spared to make the camp attractive. No accommodation is

provided for women
workers, who were, in
1975, having to camp

Below: More traditional
Shetland scene

Mrs Spence, the assistant planning officer, told me: 'We've slowed things down to give the community time to adjust.' There has been pressure for bigger service bases with more berths – not from the oil companies, it seems, but from the base operators. But the number of berths has been firmly limited to twenty-seven. What, I asked, would be the results of allowing bigger bases? 'The population would grow too fast,' Mrs Spence replied, 'there would be too much traffic, too much pressure on service industries, and all kinds of social problems.' The principle is: first the sports centre – and, I hope, the coffee-bars and restaurants – and then the population increase. As for allowing a refinery at Sullom Voe, the planners feel that this would be altogether too

much. They will oppose it strongly, both on social and ecological grounds.

This attitude, it seemed to me, was an intelligent response to the mixed feelings of Shetlanders about the oil boom. For it was here, more than anywhere, that I was aware of doubts going beyond the universal doubts about whether it's going to last. As usual, the division of opinion is broadly political. People of conservative outlook (with a small 'c', as they're mostly Liberal voters) are the most regretful. Labour supporters, and working-class people in general, naturally think first and foremost of jobs and wages. Labour is surprisingly strong in this non-industrial community; there was a Labour majority in Lerwick Town Council, which no longer exists since the changes in local government, and the new Shetland Council has five Labour members out of twenty-two, most of the others being independents of varying coloration. Alex Morrison, a veteran Labour Councillor, said to me emphatically: 'If it weren't for the oil we'd be in the depths, in a worse plight than before the war. We've got full employment, our men who were forced to leave their homes have come back, there's a new spirit about – why shouldn't we be glad?'

What Alex Morrison says is true, and my guess is that most Shetlanders would take the same attitude, like most people in Nigg and Aberdeen and Peterhead. (It wasn't very wise of Mrs Spence, I felt, to say that she'd advise the Council to take the issue of the refinery to a referendum; I should be surprised to see the opposition victorious.) And yet, when I speak of mixed feelings, I think not simply of a clash of opinion, but of feelings mixed within the same individual mind. The wave of the future appears, in a community unused to change, too powerful, perhaps too overwhelming, to be welcomed without some qualms. An elderly woman – a native of Edinburgh who has lived happily in the Shetlands for forty years – pursed her lips judiciously when I asked what she thought about the oil boom and replied: 'It's good for Shetland but bad for the life of Shetland.' At a glance, the statement seems confused or even absurd. It expresses, all the same, an honest hesitation between clear material benefit and less tangible loss.

There is something, I soon gathered, called 'the Shetland way of life'. My hosts, Londoners by origin, used the phrase ironically but affectionately, as though repeating a family joke. It may be a product of romantic nostalgia; it may be, and I suppose it is, employed by the satisfied to deny the aspirations of those in greater need. Nevertheless it contains, I suspect, a reality. If I am guessing right, it means a habit of self-reliance, a desire to

Supply base, Lerwick: a diver has been exploring to report on the possibility of deepening harbour

control the shape and scale of life, an agreed view of what is and what is not fitting, and a sense of being different from other people. Many Shetlanders have a vague, and some a sharp, awareness that these values are under threat.

The old woman I just mentioned said: 'You used to know everybody you met, but now you see people and wonder who they might be.' A younger woman said: 'People here never used to lock their cars, you know, but now they do. There's no doubt the crime rate has risen.' (From very low to rather less low, but all the same it has risen.) And a middle-aged man: 'They're asking people to work fourteen hours a day. What pleasure is there in that? Our folk won't do it for long.'

Councillor Edward Thomason put the case against the oil boom, making it clear that he'd be happier if it had never happened. 'Being a group of islands, the Shetlands have always been a cohesive community, and that's what we're losing. I fear that life here will soon be pretty intolerable. You often see drunks in the street; there's only one town, there's very little entertainment, these construction workers are bound to flock into Lerwick and buy bottles in the afternoons. It was a bit like this in the war, but then nobody had big money, the beer was weak, the men were under discipline, and anyway the permissive society hadn't arrived and it was normal to respect social rules. Young men are tempted by easy money, they leave the jobs they were trained for, they're working like coolies. But with prices rising, people who don't have oil jobs are worse off than before. So the whole balance is upset. A young woman I know, a nice educated girl, got a job as a secretary with a foreign firm – no, not American, European – and although the pay was good and the work was easy she gave it up;

they spoke to her as though she was a backward native. Before the oil came, you couldn't have had an experience like that. Some people say we'd have been sunk without it, but I don't accept that. We get a lot of help from the Highlands and Islands Development Board, we'd have got other new enterprises going. Now it's out of our hands.'

By intelligent planning and by mobilizing the power of the community, it may well prove possible for the Shetlands – and for each and all of the parts of Scotland touched by the oil rush – to enjoy the benefits of the 'black gold' while fending off the dangers. Yet I left the islands in thoughtful mood; and, as I end this book, I want to step out of the role of observer and reporter to make a few reflections.

Wealth alone – even if dressed up as 'growth', 'expansion', or 'progress' – cannot yield a better life for working people unless they confront it with the countervailing power of political and economic democracy. Formerly, in the Arab kingdoms and sheikhdoms, people tended camels and goats and were virtually penniless, autocrats wielded absolute power, and their subjects lacked all human rights. Today, people work in oilfields and refineries for wages of which they never dreamed, autocrats wield absolute power, and their subjects lack all human rights. Of course, Britain is an advanced country in which political freedom, mass education, public responsibility for social welfare and free trade unionism are established achievements. Nevertheless, the aspirations of ordinary men and women can be realized only by vigilance, and where necessary defiance, toward the claims of property. This is equally true whether the state has a statistical 51% share in oilfields (as indeed is the case nowadays in the Middle East) or not. Also, it is equally true whether the oil men have to deal with a British government or with an Edinburgh authority which has designated the new wealth as Scotland's oil.

It is idle to wish the oil boom out of existence, and idle to deny its obvious economic advantages. It is illusory, for reasons of investment and technical expertise, to imagine that the North Sea operation can be carried through by anyone except the great multi-national oil companies. But it is foolish – knowing what we ought to know about these companies – to expect them to give priority to social responsibility and human well-being.

As the phrase goes, they are not in business for their health. Nor yet for ours.   Lerwick